Leadership:
Self, School, Community

By Robert Maher

Division of Student Activities
National Association of Secondary School Principals

This book is dedicated to all the leadership teachers, activity advisers, and student leaders who have taken the time to "step forward and make a difference—improving the quality of life."

Robert Maher

ABOUT THE AUTHOR: Robert Maher is principal of Cornwall (N.Y.) High School

Copyright 1988
National Association of Secondary School Principals
1904 Association Dr., Reston, Va. 22091
(703) 860-0200

ISBN 0-88210-217-6

Contents

Introduction

During the spring of 1983, an article describing a course called Character Development and Leadership Training in the School and Community appeared in *Education Week*—a newspaper read by many educators. The course was one I had instituted at Lakeland High School in Shrub Oak, a middle class suburb in Westchester County, about 30 miles north of New York City. Much to my surprise, I received nearly 500 letters requesting information about the course.

In this book I will explain in some detail my reasons for starting a Character Development and Leadership Training program, the techniques I have found successful in moving it forward, the community resources that have proved valuable, and some of the problems and roadblocks I have learned to avoid. It is my hope that this book will make it unnecessary for educators eager to begin such a course to rediscover the wheel.

The program at Lakeland works. Student applications for the course continue to grow. Administrators and staff members are pleased with the role students have played in our school district, and community members have responded favorably. I am confident that other schools can enjoy the same level of success by examining and adapting to their own institutions the strategies we have used at Lakeland High School.

Character Development and Leadership Training

Judy Garland and Mickey Rooney taking time from chemistry lab and work to produce a student musical for a local charity in the old Andy Hardy movies; Archie and his friends laboring long hours to decorate the gym for the prom; the student athletes in the Clair Bee and John Tunis sports stories struggling for a victory on the football field, cheered on by apple-cheeked cheerleaders with homemade pom-pons while parent volunteers working at the hot dog stand root for the team.

There was a time not that long ago when American schools were represented by such images in the public imagination. For most Americans these images were representations of American education at its best. Schools were places where such things did go on; maybe not for everyone, but they did go on often enough to make support for education something that was taken for granted. Americans were proud of their schools.

Then, in the 1960s and 1970s, something went wrong. Andy Hardy and Archie were replaced in the taxpayers' minds by an antisocial, drug-dealing character who cut more classes than he attended in a graffiti-covered school building.

To be sure, this image was as much a caricature as the earlier, idealized version of the American school student. But there was enough truth in it to be of concern. Things were going on in the schools that would never have been tolerated in earlier years. Teachers complained as loudly as the taxpayers. Parents blamed the teachers. Teachers blamed the parents.

For the successful introduction of our Character Development and Leadership Training course, however, one other group of the community had to make its discontentment felt: the students. They too had to look at what was happening to their world and say, at least to themselves, "I am mad, and I am not going to take it anymore!"

They had to realize that the students who were disruptive were not making things miserable just for the faculty and administrators (although they certainly were doing just that). They were ruining things for the great majority of the student body.

It is an old cliché in education circles, but true nonetheless: 90 percent of the rules in a school are made for 10 percent of the student body. And every time a student from that disruptive 10 percent acts irresponsibly, another rule is likely to be written and implemented to further limit the freedom of the responsible 90 percent. Someone vandalizes a restroom, so it is locked—for everyone. A handful of students fight at an evening athletic event, so they cancel all night games. A fire alarm is pulled—and the entire student body and faculty stands for 10 minutes in the freezing mid-winter cold.

At our school vandalism and loitering in the restrooms proved to be the launching pad for the program. Students complained that the conditions were so bad many students refused to use the restrooms at all, even though they were in school for more than seven hours each day. They refused to wade through the loiterers, trash, graffiti, and cigarette smoke to get to the urinals, cracked mirrors, and stalls with broken doors.

The teachers and administrators, after hearing student complaints, could address the situation, perhaps by assigning teachers or aides to monitor each restroom. But the real challenge was for the students to come up with a better answer. Could they take the initiative and solve the problem? Could they play a role in improving things for themselves and their fellow students? Could they step forward and become leaders?

Self, School, and Community

A successful program in Character Development and Leadership Training must serve three critical needs: the improvement of self, of school, and of community. Our course attempts to meet these needs by having each student in the program analyze how he or she can best fit into a network of service organizations, first within the school (his or her immediate community as a student); in the local community (the neighborhood); and on the national and international level by association with charitable groups such as UNICEF, Muscular Dystrophy, and Guiding Eyes for the Blind.

The main objective, then, is for the students to better themselves by knowing themselves and what kinds of leadership roles they are best suited to perform; and to better the school as an educational and social community so that the student body will encounter a healthy and supportive atmosphere for their growth as scholars and persons. The final phase is for the students to become involved in established community organizations.

Of course, it would be unrealistic to expect the program's impact to be as great or as measurable in these outside activities as within the school itself. However, through these community projects the students take the first steps toward the roles they will later play as adult members of our society. Of course, all these activities take place under the supervision and direction of a teacher.

What we aspire to is both a horizontal and a vertical development. The students seek to know and improve themselves as individuals through classroom exercises, readings, and activities; they become involved with committees charged with specific tasks to improve the school; they are responsible for committing to an individual project, and to a community project. All these activities are separate undertakings, vertical projects with a purpose of their own.

But, the student's self-development will be thwarted by a school in disarray. A school with difficulties will only be supported in its efforts to improve itself by a community of taxpayers that views the student body in a favorable light, the kind of favorable light likely to be thrown upon students working to end world hunger, teaching Sunday School, volunteering in local nursing homes, collecting food and toys for orphans, and organizing blood drives. Thus, the horizontal connection—the integration of self, school, and community. One cannot be what one ought to be without the support of others.

Student Selection

The process through which the members of the class are screened and selected is of critical importance. If the class is perceived unfavorably by the faculty, community, or student body, or if the members of the class perform unacceptably in their community projects, the result would be counterproductive.

How many students should be in the program? Initially, members should represent no more than 10-20 percent of the student population.

Consideration should be given to upperclassmen for two reasons: First, it is easier to find room for the course in a school's schedule as an elective. Second, upperclassmen are generally the student body leaders by virtue of their age and experience. (At Lakeland we have also found the course to be a good remedy for what we all know as "senioritis.")

This is not to say that elements of the program cannot be added to the general curriculum or expanded to reach underclassmen after a year or two. The self-analysis, the introduction to community and charitable work, the awakening of a sense of responsibility for those less fortunate than ourselves—all these things would be beneficial to the entire student body. But the committee work involved in the program must be limited to a number supervisable by the teacher. Twenty to 25 students per class is the maximum that I would suggest.

I recommend that teachers not limit their attention to the students actually registered for the program. All members of the student body should be "scouted" as potential student leaders. It is important that the candidates not be strangers to those making the final decision about admission to the class. If students have been observed in a variety of situations in the classroom, on the athletic field, in student government, it will lessen the chance of a poor choice being selected as a member of the group simply on the basis of a good interview; or worse, a stellar candidate being passed over because of a poor interview.

The class works best as a full-year elective. In fact, the course is a 15 or 16-month undertaking.

Applications are filed in the late winter by students who wish to be considered for the following September. While the class does not begin until the following fall, those selected begin their responsibilities immediately. They organize a major spring benefit or charitable activity under the supervision of the students who are about to complete the program.

Hence, each student will have the experience of supervising younger students, of showing them the ropes, of acting as "leader of leaders." In addition, several summer workshop/training sessions ensure that the new class will be ready to go into action in September.

But before any of these activities can begin it is necessary to make sure that the right students have been chosen; that the class has the right "chemistry." Our goal from the very beginning has been to ensure that the class represents the *entire* spectrum of the student body.

The following figures are, of course, a generalization; the breakdown is stereotypical. Yet, as with most stereotypes there is an element of truth to it. It has long been my feeling (and I think few would strongly disagree) that any given class of high school students can be categorized as:

    15 percent—cream of the crop
    20 percent—good kids
    50 percent—silent majority
    15 percent—turned off kids

By "silent majority" I mean those who can be swayed to behave most admirably or into disruptive ways. The "turned off" group includes students who have a history of serious disciplinary problems in the school.

Naturally, these segments of the student body will not be equally represented in the class. The applications, for one thing, tend to come in the main from the top 35 percent of the class. But if the program is to avoid the image that so often becomes attached to many student government organizations, some effort must be made to ensure that the other groups are represented.

One of the goals of the program is to turn some of the latter groups around or, at least, to lessen their negative impact and influence on the school. Some lines of communication must be opened to them in order for this to happen.

Are there dangers in giving positions of leadership and responsibility to such students? Yes, but if the situation is handled properly, not as much as one might think. Often these are students whose disruptive behavior is just a stage in their maturing process, or the result of a poor family situation. The job for the teacher is to find those whose hearts are in the right place.

The very fact that a student applies for the class or is favorably disposed to an invitation to join is a positive sign, no matter how blemished his or her record. It has been my experience that during the screening process it is more important to be on the lookout for the good students who are choosing the course for the wrong reasons.

The advantage of having access to the "turned off kids" is so great that it would be a mistake to avoid recruiting some students from this group. Given the right projects and responsibilities, the attitude of these students can be surprisingly favorable. These students are part of a school's clientele, and little can be accomplished without, at least, their acquiescence.

The only prerequisite we stress is the determination to improve self, school, and community, to "count," and to "make a difference." No experience is necessary, only desire and commitment. In the adult world it is not only one-time honor students who operate businesses, chair charitable funds, head fraternal organizations, run political parties, labor unions, and chambers of commerce. Why, then, should there be only one type of teenager thought appropriate for positions of responsibility in a school community?

The actual screening consists of a series of interviews conducted by the teacher, along with the present members of the class. The qualities the interviewers should seek to uncover are a genuine commitment, perseverance, and a determination to serve through learning and leading. The interviewers should inquire about volunteer work previously undertaken by the candidates, either at the school or with their church or synagogue, Boy Scouts, Girl Scouts, etc.

The candidates should be asked about their reasons for applying to the class. A major part of the interviewer's job at this point is to spot the candidates who are giving the "right" answers only because they think they are the responses the interviewer wants to hear. The candidates' school records should be reviewed. In some cases the candidates' teachers, or administrators, may be queried about incidents that might work for and/or against the student. One cannot be too thorough at this stage. A poorly selected class will cause a year of headaches for everyone involved.

At the end of the screening a group slightly larger than the intended class size should be chosen. The assumption is that there will be dropouts during the project assignment the group undertakes that spring, or during the summer training workshops. The course is not a frill; nor is it an easy grade. There are other courses that students can select that will make their school year less demanding academically. Character Development and Leadership Training is not meant to be one of them. Once that idea sinks in, certain students may change their minds about the attractiveness of the course.

It is enlightening—often truly surprising—to watch the new candidates go into action for the first time with the spring project. Unexpected attitudes pop to the surface. Some students show unanticipated levels of competence, creativity, independence, and determination. Unfortunately, some others begin to display tendencies toward shirking responsibilities.

A blood drive at Lakeland is an example of a spring project: The local blood bank was contacted about suitable dates. A site for the actual donations was chosen by a committee, after consultation with the school administrators. Another committee worked on publicity, making posters, contacting local radio stations, making announcements, and distributing pamphlets.

Arrangements were made to secure the custodial help needed to set up and break down the donation site. A refreshment committee made arrangements. A sign-up committee secured the required forms.

Regular meetings were held to coordinate the work. Reports were given to the teacher and to the other committees. Occasionally the mentor students met the teacher to assess the "performance under pressure" of the new enrollees. Opportunities were sought for the mentors or for the teacher to give leads, correct errors, or rally the group.

The Leadership Application

All students applying to be accepted into the Character Development and Leadership Training program should be aware that:

A. Acceptance assumes

1. Complete involvement and dedication of time and effort. Willingness to spend time in school, after school, and during vacations for completion of projects.

2. Enrollment in the class and fulfillment of requirements.

3. Exhibiting leadership qualities in all roles in realization of this select honor.

4. Utilizing communication skills in dealing with community, school personnel, and students.

5. Spending time working on leadership skills in summer workshops.

6. Passing all courses.

B. The interview process will include:

1. An application that will be turned in to the teacher before the interview.

2. A 250 word essay on "Why You Feel You Should Be Chosen To Be Part of the Class."

3. A two-part interview involving questions about your views of leadership, school, and community.

4. Acceptance and notification.

Application

Name _____ Date _____

Address _____

Phone _____ Period _____ Room No. _____

Schools you have attended:

Elementary _____

Address _____

Middle School _____

Address _____

High School Other Than Present High School

_____

Address _____

School activities you have been involved in:

Activity   Year

_____

_____

_____

_____

_____

Community clubs, organizations, and sports you have been involved in: .

_____

_____

_____

_____

What is your probable overall average for this year? _____

What is your favorite course in school? _____

_____

What are your plans for after high school? _____

Travel _____ Work _____ College _____

Other _____

What is your career goal? _____

_____

Interview Comment Sheet

Interviewer _____

Prospective Student _____

_____

What was your general reaction to the interview? _____

_____

_____

Would you recommend this person for the class?

Yes _____   No _____

Why? _____

_____

Are there any reservations about this person? If so, please explain:

_____

_____

_____

Ideas for interviewing prospective leadership students

Stress:

1. Time commitment—willingness to give up free periods, evenings, lunch, etc.

2. Priorities—willingness to make this one of your top priorities.

3. Responsibility is on student to make the most of the class.

4. Involvement in committees—importance of choosing a committee you will like.

5. Volunteer work.

6. Negative aspects—stereotype of always selling for trip, getting out of class, teacher complaints, etc.

7. Creative ability—if you cannot come up with what you want done, must be willing to carry out others' plans.

***** Questions *****

1. What makes one worthy of being in the class?

2. What have you heard about the class?

3. What would you like to see done in the school?

4. What would be the most important thing you might get out of the class?

5. What do you expect the class to be like?

6. What do you consider a good leader to be like?

7. What type of experiences have you had that would help you in this role?

8. Would you be willing to speak in front of an audience, group of students, friends about the program?

9. What is the most important thing students should be taught at Lakeland?

10. What type of relationship should students have with teachers?

11. How do you feel about doing things for other people?

12. Could you be a good follower as well as leader?

Time Line

March 1   **Classroom Visits**

Leadership teacher and students visit classrooms to discuss the leadership class and "recruit" new candidates.

15   **Applications Due**

All leadership candidates must submit written applications about self, intent, and reason for applying.

April 1   **Interviews Begin**

All applicants are screened by leadership teacher and a committee of present leadership students.

May 1–
June 30   **Quasi-Internship Program Begins**

Present leadership students take a small group of applicants and lead them through what would be expected of them if they are accepted into the course. Heavy emphasis on individual and group projects.

July 1   **Summer Workshops**

Teacher and students meet once a week in an informal setting (beach, park, grassy spot) and conduct value clarification/self-actualization type workshops. Near the end of summer, a goodbye and good luck party is thrown for the recent graduates.

September 1   **Opening Day Barbecue**

Leadership class hosts a "Welcome Back to School" event for all staff.

September 1–
April 30   **Formal Classes**

Classes are conducted five days per week (42-minute periods); however, the majority of the work really is completed before and after school and during free time.

Sample Exercises and Descriptions

In the early weeks of the fall semester, students undertake an in-depth self-analysis and go through the first in a series of inspirational and motivational readings.

The students are encouraged to confront character traits and short-comings that prevent them from maximizing their potential, first as individuals, then as leaders.

We have found several techniques effective in helping the students confront themselves in an honest and forthright manner. We have also found several exercises that help the students deal with the dynamics and pressures involved in assuming a leadership role; others help promote effective decision making. Some of these are described on the following pages.

Getting Acquainted

Find someone who . . .   Signature and School

1. Is left handed.   _____

2. Plays a brass musical
   instrument.   _____

3. Has a picture of their pet with
   them.   _____

4. Has a hole in their stocking or
   sock.   _____

5. Wears green contact lenses.   _____

6. Has on preppie clothes.   _____

7. Was born outside the United
   States.   _____

8. Has almost the same color of
   hair as you.   _____

9. Is the tallest person in the
   group.   _____

10. Has the same last initial as you. _____

11. Has a birthday in July. _____

12. Knows how to ride a horse. _____

13. Plans to be a teacher. _____

14. Has a teddy bear for a friend. _____

15. Can name the last 10 U.S. Presidents. _____

16. Likes to sail. _____

17. Can name Santa's eight reindeer. _____

18. Has pierced ears. _____

19. Is on a diet. _____

20. Is a guitar player. _____

21. Has collected more than 50 LP albums. _____

22. Has a toothbrush in their pocket/purse. _____

23. Recycles aluminum or paper. _____

24. Likes to camp in the wilderness. _____

25. Exercises more than one hour a day. _____

26. Reads more than one book a month. _____

27. Has never been to Washington, D.C. _____

28. Rides a bike to school. _____

I am looking for someone who:

1. Plays the piano _____

2. Has the middle name Jane _____

3. Won a varsity letter _____

4. Has been in an amateur play _____

5. Has been a volunteer worker _____

6. Has a birthmark on his/her leg _____

7. Did not see *E. T.* _____

8. Has been to a ballet performance _____

9. Has never flown in a plane _____

10. Has green eyes _____

11. Runs at least two miles a day _____

12. Is a downhill skier _____

13. Is an only child _____

14. Has been in the same room with a U.S. president _____

15. Is a Capricorn _____

16. Has more than five brothers and sisters _____

17. Speaks two languages _____

18. Has lost 20 pounds this past year _____

19. Can name the seven dwarfs _____

20. Is fond of pizza with the works, including anchovies _____

21. Gets up earlier than 9:00 a.m. on Sunday morning _____

22. Would like to be a contestant on "Wheel of Fortune" _____

Life Collage

The students are asked to put together a collage that will effectively portray the high and low points and shaping influences in their lives. Our experience has been that the students undertake this task with an amazing degree of honesty and candor. They will portray unpleasant incidents—deaths, moral failures—as well as their proudest moments.

What results is a single artistic representation of who they are and the forces that helped mold their personalities, beliefs, convictions, fears, anxieties, and insecurities. The hope is that, in the process of putting together and interpreting the collage, the students will see themselves more clearly.

Does it work? I think so. The students say so. They begin to talk of an interrelatedness of the events of their lives which they had not confronted before. They also begin to see in the pictures on each other's collages what it is that leads to the differences and similarities within the group: wedding pictures, large and small family photos, First Communions, Bar and Bat Mitzvahs, funerals, awards, pictures of athletic achievements, etc.

Personal Diary

The students are encouraged to take stock of their lives on a regular basis, to make a record of their accomplishments on a daily basis to see if they are progressing as leaders, spinning their wheels, or perhaps falling back into old and self-destructive patterns of behavior. Since one of the basic questions the students are expected to ask themselves is "Where am I going?" they should, in the pages of this diary, be able to see something they can point to with pride, or to question their actions.

Favorites

Some class time is spent on an analysis of each student's favorite song. Since much modern popular music, especially rock, features songs with a message or image, this exercise works quite well. Why does one student hate disco with such passion? Why has another decided she prefers jazz to the rock she used to love so much? Why has another found out that country music is much more to his taste than punk rock? Why do so many of them feel compelled to wear T-shirts that ensure everyone else knows of their choice? Why does a particular ballad have such a prominent place in someone's life?

A similar exercise centers on a discussion of what animal would best represent each member of the class. What animal would they pick to become if such a choice became necessary? Why? Do the other members of the class think another beast a more appropriate representation? Why?

Naturally this exercise usually leads to a good deal of good-natured ribbing among the students, which is fine. It works. Students who wish to be lions or panthers are saying something about themselves that is worthwhile for them to confront. As are those who prefer to be sleepy old steers sitting in the shade, or those who think they would be best represented as tigers when the rest of the class thought they would pick a jellyfish. Later, after the laughter has subsided and the students have a change to reflect on their own about what took place, valuable insights will occur.

NAME _____

Where born and raised

Favorite song

Favorite town

What you like best in others

Place you'd like to visit

A person you highly respect

Three words that best describe you

One or two things you really value

Favorite book and movie

Something that made you feel good today

19

NAME _____ DATE _____

What I'd like to learn more about _____

_____

_____

What I don't care to learn more about _____

_____

_____

What I like best _____

_____

_____

What I like least _____

_____

_____

What I think I'd like to be when I grow up _____

_____

_____

The most interesting thing I've done in my life is _____

_____

_____

One of the happiest days in my life has been _____

_____

_____

My three best friends are _____

_____

_____

If I could make three wishes and have them come true they would be:

_____

_____

_____

If I Were A ?

If I were an animal, I'd like to be a _____

because _____.

If I were a toy, I'd like to be a _____

because _____ .

If I were a food, I'd like to be a _____

because _____ .

If I were a grown up, I'd like to be _____

because _____ .

If I were in the circus, I'd like to be the _____

because _____ .

If I were a famous star, I'd like to be _____

because _____ .

If I were a gift, wrapped in a bright red ribbon, I'd like to be a _____

_____

because _____ .

If I were a piece of clothing, I'd like to be a _____

because _____ .

If I could be anything in the whole world, I'd like to be a

_____

because _____

_____

_____

_____

_____

The Best

The best person in the world is _____

_____ .

The best food I have ever eaten is _____

_____ .

The best TV show I have ever seen is _____

_____ .

The best movie I have ever seen is _____

_____ .

I have the best time when I'm _____

_____ .

The best thing about school is _____

_____ .

The best thing about me is _____

_____ .

The best thing I can think of is _____

_____ .

The best idea I've ever had was _____

_____ .

The best thing about my family is _____

_____ .

The best teacher I've ever had was _____

_____ .

The best present I've ever received was _____

_____ .

My best memory is _____

_____ .

My best friend is _____ .

The Worst

The worst thing that has ever happened to me was _____

_____

_____

_____ .

The worst food in the world is _____

_____ .

The worst show on TV is _____

_____ .

The worst movie I have ever seen is _____

_____ .

The worst thing about school is _____

_____ .

The worst song I have ever heard was _____

_____ .

The worst thing about my life is _____

_____ .

The worst thing that I have ever done is _____

_____ .

The worst fight I have ever had was _____

_____ .

The worst thing that I can think of is _____

_____ .

It Hurts

There are many ways to feel hurt. There is the pain that you feel
when you hurt yourself, like I did when I _____

_____ .

I felt as if I was going to _____ .

Another time _____

hurt me when he (she) _____ .

The worst pain that I have ever felt happened when _____

_____ .

There is also the hurt that you feel when you are sad. I remember feeling

sad when _____ .

Another time _____

made me sad because _____

_____ .

There were times when I might have hurt someone else. I remember

once when _____

_____ .

Later, I felt _____ .

The thing that hurts the most is _____

_____ .

Here are some other things that make me feel like crying:

1. _____

2. _____

3. _____

Ten Years from Now

Ten years from now I will probably look like _____ .

I will be _____ and _____ .

Every morning I will get up and go to _____ .

When my friends see me, they will say "_____ ."

Ten years from now my family will probably _____

_____ . One member of my family

will be doing something very strange. This person is _____

_____ . Another member of my family

will be _____ . This person is

_____ .

Ten years from now my teacher, Mr. (Ms.) _____

will be _____ . When I see him (her)

on the street I will say "_____ ."

Ten years from now I will own a _____

and a _____ .

Ten years from now the world will be very different. Here are some of the things that will probably change.

1. _____

2. _____

3. _____

When I Get Married

When I grow up, I am going to marry someone just like _____

_____ . He (she) will be very

_____ and _____ .

He (she) will not act like _____ .

When I get married, I will live in _____

and have a _____

and a _____ .

I will have _____ children. Two of their names will be

_____ and _____ , and they will be very _____ .

If I decide not to get married, it will be because _____

_____ . From what I can tell, the worst things

about marriage are _____

and _____ .

But there are some good things about it too, such as _____

_____ and _____ .

As soon as I get married, I will tell my husband (wife) three things. This is what I will say:

1. "_____ ."

2. "_____ ."

3. "_____ ."

If I were old enough to get married right now, I might marry ____
_____. He (she) would be a good person to marry because _____.

Cue-Card Perception

This is an interesting training session, and one that we find quite productive. The exercise is based upon the fact that a successful leader must know how to "read" the group he or she is attempting to direct. Are they responding the way he hoped? Are they enthusiastic? Openly hostile? Quietly indifferent? Is there another approach that would work better with the group? The object of the exercise is to sharpen the student's ability to spot the varying responses.

The method we use is to have each student report to the assembled class on one of the committee projects. While the report is being delivered, cue-cards are held up so that the group receiving the report can view them, but the student delivering the report cannot. The cue-cards give a variety of instructions: e.g., "ignore me," "tease me," "humor me," "argue with me," etc.

It must be emphasized to the group receiving the report that they must not overact if this activity is to be effective. They cannot allow themselves to become caricatures of the attitudes they are seeking to express. Otherwise it will be too obvious to the student delivering the report. The reporting student's task is to see if he or she can spot listener reactions comparable to those they actually will encounter when their committee work begins; to see if he or she is getting the point across; if he or she is able to discern whether he or she is being listened to or merely heard. Can the student key on the audience's response and alter the delivery to bring the group around?

Pressure Tests

After the course has been in session for a month or two it is worthwhile to put the student leaders through the wringer a bit. Since one of the key attributes of a successful leader is the presence of mind required to perform with grace, composure, and effectiveness under pressure, some way must be found to help them confront the need not to panic when things get heated.

A mock crisis can be created in the classroom as a testing ground. One such "crisis" I have found effective is to come to class one day with an unannounced test, which I tell the class has been ordered by the district superintendent in response to community complaints that the class is a "social club" with no academic requirements. I proceed to produce a test on our class readings that is unreasonably demanding, and, with a great show of dismay and a string of protests that "my hands are tied," I inform the class that the test results are going to have to be used for a substantial portion of their upcoming report card grade.

Images of permanently scarred grade transcripts being sent to the colleges that they are hoping to attend, lowered class rank, and short-circuited career plans begin to float past the students' eyes. You can actually see it in many of their faces.

As you might expect, the immediate responses vary: anger, despair, resignation, some brooding. But some of the class show their mettle. They begin to act with character, as leaders. They take the bait and begin to seek a reasonable way out of the dilemma. They remain calm and ask the teacher to organize with them to make an appeal to the sense of reasonableness and fair play of those in the district office who are acting in what appears to be such an irrational manner.

The next portion of the period is spent in setting up the strategy and tactics for our appeal. The last 10 or so minutes are reserved for telling the students the truth and having them analyze why they performed, or failed to perform, under the gun. Those who responded in a less-than-satisfactory manner profit most of all. They failed to come through in a mock situation where that failure hurt neither themselves nor anyone else. It is hoped that they will learn from that shortcoming and be able to turn things around when the chips are really on the line.

By the time these class exercises are completed our hope is that the leadership students will have:

1. Developed a better understanding of how others perceive them and why
2. Acquired "listening" rather than "hearing" techniques
3. Learned how to deal with others, individually and collectively
4. Learned how to make a good decision and live with the results
5. Learned the art of persuasion and influence
6. Learned how to stand up for their principles in the face of unfavorable reactions.

A future leader is someone who has acquired most of the above traits and the will to use them at the appropriate time. There are many who have leadership potential, but only a few who realize and accept the challenge.

Daily Priorities

Yesterday is but a dream, tomorrow is only a vision. But today well lived makes every yesterday a dream of happiness, and every tomorrow a vision of hope. Look well, therefore, to this day.

— From the Sanskrit

Sunday

_____

_____

_____

_____

_____

_____

Monday

_____

_____

_____

_____

_____

_____

Tuesday

_____

_____

_____

_____

_____

_____

Wednesday

_____

_____

_____

_____

_____

Thursday

_____

_____

_____

_____

_____

_____

Friday

Saturday

Weekly Goals/Plans

_____ to _____

Whether you believe you can do a thing or believe you can't, you are right.

— *Henry Ford*

1. _____

2. _____

3. _____

4. _____

5. _____

6. _____

7. _____

8. _____

9. _____

10. _____

11. _____

12. _____

13. _____

14. _____

15. _____

16. _____

Lifetime Goals

Whatever the mind of man can conceive and believe, it can achieve.

My lifetime goals are:

Career

_____

_____

Financial

_____

_____

Mental and Spiritual

_____

_____

_____

Physical

_____

_____

Social and Emotional

_____

_____

_____

Committees in Action

Once again, each student is responsible for two committee experiences during the course of the program: an in-school committee assigned to a specific school betterment task, and a committee assigned to a group project undertaken by the class as a whole. (In addition, each student must work on his or her individual community-action project.)

It is in reference to the in-school committees that the most questions usually arise. "What kinds of things do the students *do*?" people frequently ask. The committees that seem to work best at our school include: announcements, bulletin boards, career awareness, newspaper, cable TV and radio, and supervisory or school watch.

Each of these committees deals with the overall betterment of the school in interlocking roles. The students select the committee they decide is best suited for their talents and dispositions. They serve on this committee from May of their junior year through April of their senior year, then as advisers to the new Leadership group from May until they graduate. The committee's members are expected to report to the class on a regular basis in a formal, coherent, and prepared manner, much as would be expected in a business or professional organization.

Announcement Committee

This committee writes, edits, and delivers all intra-school announcements: birthdays, club and sports announcements, important events, activity preludes, thoughts-for-the-day/week, plus the fundamental building news. This means that all copy for the announcements is turned in to them, including copy from teachers and heads of organizations. In our building these announcements take place during the homeroom period at the beginning of the school day. They are delivered in "town-crier" form—with a student going to each homeroom. We find this much more effective than using the school's P.A. system.

Great care is taken to ensure that the announcements will cover the broad spectrum of activities and interests of the student body. They must not take on the appearance of being private communiques for an "in group." The goal is to initiate and encourage school spirit, as well as to inform. Catchy, peppy, funny, sometimes musical, announcements are produced to set an up-beat and positive mood for the school day, to make the student body feel good about itself, and to encourage students to participate in the activities described.

Bulletin Boards Committee

The work of this committee is very similar to that of the Announcement Committee. In our building four or five bulletin boards were used in a haphazard fashion by whatever student organization was interested in promoting an activity. The Character Development and Leadership

Training class, after consulting with the school administration, undertook responsibility for managing these boards, plus several other new boards.

Each class (senior, junior, sophmore, and freshman) was assigned a board. The others were allotted to various school organizations: student government, sports and clubs, the week board, guidance board (usually college and career publicity), newspaper articles board (clippings from local newspapers about the school and student body), and the "what's happening?" board.

It is this committee's responsibility to find material suitable for each of the boards, either by clipping or drawing it themselves, or by having other students do the artwork, then to make sure it is tastefully and colorfully arranged—and that it stays this way.

The committee, in other words, is responsible for maintaining the boards: removing graffiti or improper displays, as well as changing the displays on a regular basis to ensure that each board will be up-to-date. It is stressed to this committee that their efforts should ensure that the bulletin boards are both informational and inspirational.

The effect of this work on the atmosphere of the school will be considerable. I notice it most whenever I walk through another school where the bulletin boards are not given any thought or care, where rag-tag posters from events long past are mixed with obscene graffiti and hastily scrawled notices about coming events.

It might be argued that a bulletin board is an insignificant feature of a school, hardly worth great concern; but I don't think the argument would be pressed if anyone could see the difference in atmosphere in a building where the bulletin boards create an image of a school where good things are going on, where people care. Bulletin boards are quite often the first things that catch the eye of a visitor to a school.

Cable TV and Radio Committee

A few years back it would have been unreasonable to suggest that a group of high school students go out and produce a monthly television program. In some large metropolitan areas the birth of the cable television industry has changed this situation. For the foreseeable future a good number of the cable television stations will be looking for suitable programming to fill their air time, especially in the non-prime-time hours. And what better to suggest to them than a show with a built-in audience, an audience of a good number of the local high school students and their parents? We call our show "Lakeland High School in the News."

But where will you find students with the required expertise? There really is no problem here. The local cable operators will provide the essentials, the technical assistance, the training required. Surprisingly, it takes only a few hours to get the students ready to produce their own show.

And what will they do during the hour they are on the air? Basically, that is the committee's decision. I think you will find the students quite imaginative and creative. In all likelihood, it will be the teacher's job to winnow through the suggestions for a good show and help pick the best. Interviews with students who have achieved something out of the ordinary in the school or community, round table discussions of some school program or problem, student-produced plays, debates, and profiles of a student or teacher-of-the-month are just a few of the shows that are likely to do well.

Local radio stations are another source that can be tapped for this type of activity, either in addition to or instead of the cable television station. It is my belief that every area of the country will have some stations willing to participate in such an enterprise. A little preparation and some legwork will result in a surprising amount of goodwill and cooperation from people in the radio and television industry. After all, their business is attracting viewers and listeners. If you can convince them you have an audience for your proposed show, and if the students display some sincerity and a willingness to learn, you are home.

Tell the students on this committee to be daring, to go for it, to make it work. They cannot undertake this project on the assumption that the important people in these media simply could not be interested in a show by a bunch of kids.

Write them, call them, tell them what you have in mind. Go to the top. Contact the station manager. Don't assume that people in high positions will be unwilling to talk on the phone. They are not always too busy to listen.

The results? An ongoing public relations build-up for the school. The students begin to see their school in a different and positive light. The community hears something good about the school, and sees "good kids" doing something worthwhile, instead of the usual newspaper stories of drug busts and fights and car crashes involving students. The students on the committees benefit from what amounts to a free communications internship. You can watch their poise and polish develop with each broadcast.

Newspaper Committee

As one would expect, this committee's work is much like that of the cable TV and radio committee. The cooperation of local newspapers may come even easier than that of the television and radio stations. In fact, they usually are enthusiastic. They *do* have space—if a well-written student column is offered to them, something on a regular basis about school activities, guest speakers at the school, special programs, student trips, interviews with students who have achieved significant honors in the classroom or community work, or faculty and administration profiles.

Our students on this committee meet with the local city editors to establish guidelines. In addition to writing their own column they also agree to serve as "tipsters" on possible feature articles for the newspaper's staff reporters.

The experience this committee offers to the would-be journalist is invaluable, while providing good press for the school.

It is important for the teacher, perhaps with the assistance of an English teacher, to make sure that these columns are error-free and professional in appearance. Nothing can deaden the interest of the editor as much as sloppy and awkward writing. They know they are not dealing with Pulitzer Prize winners, but they will not respond well to copy that does not exhibit care and attention and a reasonable level of competence.

Career Awareness Committee

We have found this to be an area long neglected by the schools. Granted, students deserve a time in their lives when they are free to fantasize about unlikely careers—private detectives, movie stars, professional athletes, and the like. But it also would be beneficial if they were made aware of the nature of their more down-to-earth (and more likely) choices.

To this end, the Career Awareness Committee is responsible for investigating a variety of careers, from accounting to zoology. Each member of the committee is assigned to a number of careers, usually ones the student is considering. The committee members then research the career, contact people in the profession, and, if possible, arrange for visits to our school. They also are able to set up what we call "mini-internships" in some cases: a short taste of the job for interested students.

When members of the different professions come to the school, conferences are held, open to all members of the class and other interested seniors. The members of the committee, in addition to inviting the speaker, arrange for a suitable room for the conference, greet the speaker, and share the discussion on the day of the conference.

The culmination of the committee's work is a journal kept in the guidance department of the school. The committee members file their reports in this journal at the end of the school year. (Their grade is largely determined by the quality of their submission.) What results is an index, increasing in size with each class, of career facts and figures. It is available to the entire student body.

Individual Projects

In addition to their committee work, all students must volunteer to assist some worthwhile charitable, religious, or humanitarian group. "Wherever there is a need" is our motto.

The amount of time that must be devoted to the work varies from student to student and from volunteer activity to volunteer activity. For example, a student who volunteers to teach a Sunday school class for the year, or to work in an old age home, might very well be required to give more hours than one who agrees to work in the office of a local politician or to construct a new storage shed for the local volunteer ambulance corps. Or, perhaps it will be vice versa; it is difficult to tell in advance. This is the point: one cannot predict how much time will be required for any particular undertaking, or to judge the quality of one volunteer effort in relationship to another.

As a result, great flexibility is required when administering this portion of the course. Our policy is to require from 20 to 100 hours of volunteer work through the course of the year, to one or to a variety of charitable concerns. Up to this time, churches, synagogues, nursing homes, and work with the blind or retarded or handicapped have proven to be the most commonly chosen projects of the students in the class.

Each student reports on a regular basis to the class on the successes, failures, obstacles, stumbling blocks, keys to success, problems to avoid, interesting sidelights, and any other pertinent information he or she has encountered.

This exposure to working in the community gives great satisfaction to the participating student volunteers. By "giving something back" they discover the true joy that comes from helping others, especially those in need. They find that they truly can make a difference; that they count, and can continue to count in life.

There are also public relations benefits to be derived from this volunteer work. Community members see first-hand that the school's "products"—the young people of the area—are capable of mature and responsible and praiseworthy work.

Some of the volunteer projects are self-explanatory. As previously noted, we have had students take on the responsibility of teaching an entire Sunday school course for their church. Others have worked as teacher's aides in schools for the handicapped. Some have given their time in our own school district, going back to their middle schools and elementary schools to work as tutors.

Our local hospitals have proven to be a fertile area as well, giving our students the opportunity to work as nurses' aides and orderlies. We have several nursing homes nearby that have been more than happy to give our students a chance to bring a little happiness into the lives of their patients. They have also steered some students toward the home-bound elderly, who have been helped greatly by students who take care of the simple chores (getting the groceries, newspapers, and other odds and ends) we often take for granted.

A local chapter of Guiding Eyes for the Blind has given students an opportunity to work assisting those who train guide dogs. Homes for the retarded are in need of mature and responsible volunteers.

We have had students with skills in carpentry volunteer their time to local neighborhood improvement projects: cleaning up vacant lots, refurbishing community centers, shoring up storage sheds and recreational buildings in local parks. The possibilities are endless.

It should be mentioned that this kind of work often allows a student to experiment with a possible career choice. They get a chance to taste the atmosphere in a certain profession, and sometimes make contacts with those in the field who will be able to guide them toward the proper training.

School Watch Program

And now for the potential hornet's nest, powder keg, nightmare—call it what you will. It is the committee that brings the biggest risk, but also the greatest benefit to the school.

There are some who will be critical of the supervisory concept, faculty and students alike. It is my contention that the faculty opposition will be defused by a few months of successful work by this committee, and that those students who remain hostile are likely to be of the type that will always be hostile to authority.

We call our supervisory committee "School Watch." All members of the class are expected to cooperate in the overall responsibility of this committee, but there are some who are given specific and regular supervisory duties. For the latter group, the School Watch serves as their committee work for the year.

Drug dealing, theft, violence, and vandalism make school facilities unusable by the student body. We see no reason to be defensive about students informing on such criminal activity. The students who cooperate with the administration are no different from the courageous concerned citizens who decide to step forward at the risk of personal safety to assist the police.

Most readers will remember the famed Kitty Genovese case of a decade or so back. Kitty Genovese was the young woman killed in the streets of a residential section of New York City. Her cries for help, although heard by many of the residents, went unanswered. The middle class men of the area did nothing, later telling the police that "they did not want to get involved." Well, *they* were not stool pigeons. But neither do we wish them to be models for our student body.

School Watch is an organized effort to help better the atmosphere of our school. It seeks to provide a framework within which concerned students are able to cooperate with each other and with the staff and administration in the common effort of making the school an institution of which all can be proud. The committee members are taught that it is better to report what they see—even if their suspicions prove unfounded—than to remain quiet and risk letting a fellow student or the school become a victim.

The students on the committee are carefully and repeatedly reminded that their job is not to take action themselves, but to report what they have seen to a staff member or administrator. They are to avoid confrontations.

Members of the committee are responsible for informing the proper authorities of all suspicious activities on school grounds:

- Unauthorized visitors
- People in unsupervised areas
- Vandalism

- Breaking into or defacing lockers
- Destruction of school furniture or property
- Graffiti in restooms
- Loitering in restrooms.

What about the danger of apprehended students seeking retribution? The danger is not as great as one might think, especially if the group comprises the cross-section discussed in an earlier chapter, and if the students reporting serious infractions can be ensured anonymity.

Let us look at the importance of the cross-section first: With representation from the major segments of the student body, the impression can be avoided that the "informing" is taking place through one clique of students at the expense of others. The "informing" instead is seen as being directed against those who act in a way that ruins things for everybody in the school.

Also, if some effort has been made to get physically convincing students (athletes, for example) into the program, when the time comes to deal with a situation, the student's authority is enhanced in the way all youngsters understand.

Let me give an example.

When the graffiti and loitering problem in the restrooms was first tackled, a group of Leadership students actually went into the restrooms where these problems were evident. They approached the smokers and loiterers and simply said something to the effect of "Hey, we don't want to cause trouble, but you guys are ruining this place for everybody. Look at the mess. There are kids who won't even come in here anymore. Why don't you hang out someplace else?"

Reasonable words. Neither threatening nor inflammatory. Nevertheless *much* more effective when being spoken by a group with two football players or kids from the local car club than by a group consisting of two librarians' aides and a debater. Our conviction is that, if properly organized, the students can project an image of strength (in the good sense of that word), and of commitment.

The question of anonymity does arise, however, when we are involved with more serious infractions, especially those of a criminal nature. Will not the police demand that the informants testify publicly?

It is here that the teacher, in cooperation with the administration, must carry the ball. The way we have handled the problem is by *assuring*, without equivocation, those who inform on criminal activity that their information will *not* be used as proof, but *as a means* to secure proof of guilt. For instance, information about who is dealing drugs in the building, and where, is used only in a most confidential manner.

We use the student's information only as a guide to our own surveillance. It is only when we catch the drug dealer in the act, either dealing or in possession, that we apprehend him or her and call the police. Only the administrator and the teacher are aware of why they kept such a careful eye on the student who was apprehended.

There are a certain number of the class who go even further with their supervisory responsibilities. They make supervision their specific committee responsibility, just as some others choose bulletin boards or radio work. This undertaking requires that the students become responsible for a hall duty assignment during the year, either on a permanent basis for one class period each day, or as a substitute for absent staff.

These students actually undertake the duties of a hall monitor for that post: e.g., keeping the halls clear during classes, checking the restrooms for loiterers, directing hall movement to the proper corridors, etc. Needless to say, those involved must be carefully trained to avoid physical confrontations, or to handle them properly if unavoidable.

Not all supervisory work is within the realm of surveillance and apprehension, however. The committee also seeks preventive measures, activities designed to occupy the time and attention of those who otherwise might be involved in vandalism or worse. Regular showings of movies during the lunch periods, complete with a class-operated popcorn stand, is one such activity.

The committee members choose movies they think will draw an audience, rent the films, and find a suitable site for the showings on a daily basis. A portion of the movie is repeated during the last half of each of our school's lunch periods, so that a student can eat lunch in a reasonable amount of time, get to the film, and see the entire movie over the course of a week or so.

At first, some staff members protested that a school day was no place for video cassettes of *Rocky* and *Star Wars,* but the sight of known lunchtime troublemakers sitting attentively in the film room each day brought a change of heart in most cases.

Special Projects

All our special projects are administered in much the same way as our blood bank, described earlier. The teacher's responsibilities are basically those of an organizer and coordinator, guaranteeing that there is a proper division of labor among the students in the class.

The exact details of that division of labor will depend on the type of fundraiser being launched. There is a difference between organizing a car wash at a local gas station in order to raise money for the school band, and sponsoring a basketball game between the faculty and the New York Yankees to raise money for a local charity.

The fundraisers most likely to succeed will vary, depending upon the time of the year and the area of the country. Listed below are some of the projects that have worked for us in our area of the country. Literally thousands of dollars have been raised each year by our classes through undertakings such as these.

Spare-a-Bite Program

Through a month-long promotion—posters, announcements, handouts—students are encouraged to donate the cost of one "skipped" meal to aid world hunger. The money is chanelled to UNICEF. This United Nations agency will provide posters and advice about the best way to organize the effort.

Muscular Dystrophy Sports Games

Softball and basketball games are held, pitting the school faculty and student body against local professional athletes, radio and television celebrities, and local police officers. Usually all it takes to get the cooperation of the sports and entertainment celebrities is a phone call. Local teams and radio and television stations will often have a desk specifically assigned to such charitable functions. Don't be bashful. Call, or have the students call.

Another successful fundraiser of this sort was a basketball game against a team from the Eastern Paralyzed Veterans Hospital.

Foster Parents Plan

Money from a variety of the Leadership fundraisers was used to support an orphan from another country—a most rewarding activity for the class. The agencies involved in such work arrange for pictures of the adopted child, as well as having the child write to the members of the class. The usual arrangement is for the agency to set an amount to be donated per month to cover the child's basic support.

Holiday Toy Drive

During the Christmas/Hannukah season the student body is encouraged, through the usual vehicles of posters and announcements during the homeroom period, to bring in a toy. The class hires a truck to transport the toys, and a group from the class oversees the distribution to the proper charitable institutions.

Prom Night "Hot-Line"

Through this committee's work we attempt to avoid the tragedies that all too often result from prom night drinking and driving. First of all, we encourage the students not to drink on prom night. The committee also provides students with an alternative to a dangerous ride home. They set up a network of parents and responsible alumni who are willing to come out, even in the wee hours, to drive home anyone who finds himself or herself in a questionable situation.

The students attending the prom are assured that no questions will be asked. A promise of no recriminations is given. No tales will be told. Each student attending the prom is given a card with a phone number when they receive their prom bids. The number is also prominently displayed at the prom itself. A call to that number will get them the ride home they need.

While many of these activities are usually handled by the student council, service clubs, National Honor Society, etc., the key difference here is that academic lessons are prepared to introduce the importance and relevance of each topic. A follow-up discussion on the activity also occurs to improve next year's attempt.

The Summer Break

Some might question whether the summer workshops are really all that necessary. After all, they do place unique demands on both the teacher and the class. What about vacations? Summer jobs?

Character Development and Leadership Training development are different. They require a commitment different from virtually any other course. Team spirit is required to make it work. I attribute much of our success to the camaraderie and understanding of self and school needs developed in our summer workshops.

First of all, the summer workshops need not be unpleasant or a burden to those involved. Nor must they take place in a classroom. Quite the contrary. I suggest, in fact, that they are better if they do not. Picnics, softball games, and beach parties provide a much better atmosphere for the process I have in mind.

We seek an informal, relaxed atmosphere, a period when a serious pursuit of self-awareness and values clarification can take place.

"Relax and Perfect" is the phrase we use at these gatherings. The new enrollees are encouraged to examine what is happening to their lives.

Are they proud of the type of young American they are becoming? How is their present behavior and level of accomplishment going to affect their adult life?

They are quickly leaving the stage of their lives where failures can be explained away with the plea that they are "just kids." Can they avoid in the future the pitfalls that have been holding them back from realizing their full potential? Do they recognize those pitfalls when they see them? What turns are they taking along the road of life?

And what about our school? Is it doing all it can to help them face the challenges of college and the world of work? If it is not, what can be done?

In many cases, the students have a clearer picture of what is going wrong than anyone else. Where can improvements be made? How much blame lies at the doorstep of the student body? Where has a lack of student responsibility and initiative been to blame for the school's shortcomings?

What new programs or facilities can be instituted to make things better? How can student leaders assist the administration and faculty in making the needed changes?

Group discussions are encouraged on all these topics. What is holding our school back from becoming the best in the state? How can this group point the school in that direction?

Naturally, there could be some scoffing at the idea of "best in the state." Us? Come on!

If such a reaction occurs, either at the summer workshops or in the early class sessions, it should be seized upon as an optimum teachable moment. Positive thinking should be stressed. Negativism should be characterized as something that holds back progress; that keeps us mediocre, luke-warm, complacent; that keeps us from becoming effective leaders.

The students should be reminded that Rome was not built in a day; that measurable improvements often take years; that even minimal improvements, laying the foundation, are critically important. A journey of a thousand miles begins with a single step.

It is important, by the way, for the teacher to remember that a negative or defeatist reaction is not uncommon at first, even with students who go on to experience great success in the course. The prospect, for example, of phoning community leaders, celebrities, newspaper editors, television stations, can lead to a disconcerted "Who me? What should I say?"

The responsibility of coordinating perhaps a dozen or more committees and dealing with teachers on the new level required in the program can appear overwhelming to someone who has never undertaken anything more complicated than cleaning up his or her own room.

It is for this reason that initial projects, especially the individual tasks, should be carefully chosen to ensure some initial success for the students. A confidence builder should be sought. Even later on, in the more ambitious undertakings, it is a good idea to set recognizable short-term goals along the road to the project's overall end so that the students can experience success.

Give them a feeling that they are getting somewhere. Using our blood drive, once again, as an example: Make the successful contact with the blood bank officials step one; the agreement for a suitable site in the school building step two; etc. In other words create a mood of "Okay, that's been taken care of now. We're on our way. What's next?"

By the time the summer workshops are over, the members of the class should know each other and have developed a basic trust in each other as "team players." They should have a confidence that they can make things happen for the better come fall. They should have a clear idea of some changes they want to effect in the coming school year, some problem areas they want to attack.

They also should have taken stock of themselves and come to grips with what they have to offer the school community, and what it is in their personalities that is standing in the way of their making that contribution.

These achievements are reinforced by trips scheduled during the school year. Our hope is that the students will be able to get away from the usual routine and take stock of the group's progress. How close are they coming to the goals they set for themselves during the summer?

The Teacher

The question frequently arises: What kind of teacher is required for a course such as this? Not all good teachers can do the job.

There are two things required of the Leadership teacher: extra time and role modeling.

The extra time required is considerable: the summer workshops, the after school and evening functions, community contacts, the supervision of those students involved in charitable projects. How can a teacher be expected to accept such responsibilities?

In some cases, there simply will be no problem. There will be teachers willing to give the time. There are teachers who, for a variety of reasons, have no objection to spending more hours at the school than do others. There are coaches who call more practices than they are required to call, directors of school plays who call extra rehearsals, math teachers who provide extra help each day.

There are, however, other excellent prospects who cannot, or will not, give the extra time without some compensation. In some cases imaginative scheduling can be the answer. Perhaps the teacher can be freed from the usual supervisory and chaperon duties; perhaps he or she can be given one less period to teach; perhaps extra money can be budgeted for the extra hours devoted to the course.

The teacher's leadership qualities are more difficult to describe. Not all leaders are the same; nor are all leadership teachers. Does the teacher have to be young? Female? Male? Outgoing? Sociable? No, but some qualities would seem to be essential.

The teacher must be a role model for the work and commitment expected from the students in the class. He or she cannot be a clock-watcher, willing to give only what is absolutely required. The teacher must be available to help, must be upbeat, optimistic about the possibilities of bringing about worthwhile change.

The teacher must enjoy being with young people in an informal setting, since long hours in such conditions are going to be part of the program. The teacher must be resourceful, since the projects undertaken by the class are going to have to be constructed to fit the student body and the community. The teacher must have a commitment to improving the community and the school, to making the world a better place in which to live.

The teacher must be supportive, be a dependable resource, a guide, and a counselor. The students must be encouraged to make the required phone calls, write the needed letters, consult the right authorities. If they shrink from these duties and expect the teacher to do the work, they are not being trained to be leaders.

Grading

There is no "official" grading system for the course, just as there is no required grading system for history or science courses. A standard letter or numerical grade could be attached to tests on the course readings and other written work, and to the individual charitable work and committee projects.

I "negotiate" the value of individual volunteer and charitable work with the students. In September, we project how much time they will have to give and how much responsibility they will have to assume in their project, and give it a letter grade.

Five weeks into the course each student and I hold a mini-conference to discuss progress. At the end of the 10-week period—when the first report card grade is given—the students must convince me that they have done enough to warrant the agreed-upon grade. More often than not, the students "low ball" their efforts and I end up trying to convince them of their real worth. This grade is then factored in with the grade assigned to their classwork and committee work—again, based on agreed upon goals.

Contractor Grade

Leadership is doing
  Leadership is working hard to achieve a goal
    Leadership is completing a task without supervision
      Leadership is not for everyone.

To help out the committee structure and to make the leaders and Leadership the success that it could be—the following will begin immediately:

1. Each student will be responsible for a specific task (within the committee structure)—it will be completed on a weekly basis with the results given to _____ .
(teacher)

2. If the group is involved in a project—all participants will be expected to share equally in the work and responsibility.

3. The above will be the sole determining factor for the grade given to this semester course.

The success or failure of any organization (but particularly one such as Leadership) is dependent upon the effort and hard work of each member. A chain is only as strong as its weakest link.

NAME _____

COMMITTEE _____

As a member of the above committee, I will now be expected to do the following:

_____

_____

_____

Use the back of this paper for additional comments when using an actual contract.

Grade Contracted for   A   B   C
(circle one)

Student Signature _____

Teacher Signature _____

Readings and Films

A significant portion of the in-class course time is devoted to an analysis of a series of readings and films chosen to acquaint the class with how successful men and women have viewed the key elements of Character Development and Leadership Training in their lives. Some of the readings and films focus on the techniques of leadership; others might be called motivational or inspirational—uplifting poems or epigrams, essays and short films designed to convince the students that individuals can make a difference (one of our constantly repeated themes).

These readings can be used to satisfy the traditional academic content and testing requirements for the course. Since the readings are quite often from respected works of literature, the memoirs of historic figures, or biographical sketches, their inclusion in the course also goes a long way toward defusing the objections of those who might argue that the course is not suitable for academic credit.

I would go so far as to say that, if the readings are properly chosen, the exposure to these writings, in and of itself, would constitute a respectable elective, regardless of the other activities of the group. Since many of these readings can be chosen from material in the public domain, there are few problems involved in reproducing class sets.

The following examples are meant only to give prospective teachers an idea of the reading and films that we have found appropriate in our program. Teacher preferences, availability of sources, and regional preferences will determine the selection in other school districts. But, whatever choices are presented to the students, they should satisfy two requirements: they should be uplifting and confidence-building, and they should be from respected sources.

Several of the pieces included here carry a "heavy" message. They are meant to be discussion starters. Each is meant to place each student in a thought-provoking/conflict resolution situation.

In addition we use lengthier readings, usually assigned as homework: essays, short stories, sections of biographies and autobiographies. For example: John F. Kennedy's *Profiles in Courage;* William Manchester's *The Last Lion;* Manchester's *Goodbye Darkness;* portions of James Mc-Gregor Burns' biography Franklin Delano Roosevelt; Merle Miller's recent biography of Harry Truman; the Reader's Digest's condensed version of Lawrence Elliott's *LaGuardia: Portrait of an American Original;* Charles Lindbergh's *Spirit of St. Louis; The Prophet* by Kahlil Gibran; *The Little Prince* by Antoine de Saint-Exupery; Trevor Ferrell's *Trevor's Place.*

Leadership Film List

"A Man for All Seasons"
"Captain Newman, M.D."
"Conrack"
"Freaks"
"Ghandi"
"Give 'em Hell, Harry"
"Greatest Days of Your Life . . . So Far"
"Inherit the Wind"
"Insight"
"Lilies of the Field"
"Little Big Man"
"Oh God"
"On Golden Pond"
"One Flew over the Cuckoo's Nest"
"Patton"
"Prince of the City"
"Raisin in the Sun"
"1776"
"Spartacus"
"Terms of Endearment"
"The Caine Mutiny"
"The Man Who Would Be King"
"Network"
"The Prize"
"The Color Purple"

Speech for a High School Graduate

Others will exhort you to take risks, to be yourself, never to look back or lose your faith. Not I. If the truth be told, I do not want you to take risks. Oh, maybe a selected few to preserve your self-esteem, but not the killing kind of risk, nothing netless.

As for being yourself, that's fine, as long as you are happy with yourself. Otherwise, be someone else. You'll find your way; most everyone does.

Never to look back? I'd say look back quite often. If you don't look back, you won't know it was you who smashed the china.

Never to lose faith? Of course you will. People lose their faith.

So what truth can I give you, my college-boy-to-be, on your way out? You'd think I would be able to produce something. Words are supposed to spill from writers' minds like shrimp, especially on momentous occasions like graduations, weddings, funerals. We do it all.

Instead, I reach in my desk for some verbal pocket watch to wrap up for you in tissue paper, and come up blank. Too dazed or polite, you stare at my face the way Telemachus must have stared on the beach at Ithaca, searching for Ulysses among the sailors.

Should I offer you wishes? Poets have done that for their children from time to time. In "Frost at Midnight" Coleridge wishes his son Hartley a life surrounded by nature. I could wish the same for you, though I have less trust in nature's benevolence.

Still, Mary McCarthy said something interesting in an interview recently, that "our perception of the world and our values stem absolutely from the possibility of some reasonably true perception of nature— which is gradually disappearing and will soon become impossible." That could be so. Myself, I like watching the ocean.

Yeats wished for his girl a sense of ceremony and tradition in "A Prayer for My Daughter." I'd repeat that wish for you, as long as you did not turn into a snob, like Yeats.

In "This Side of the Truth," Dylan Thomas, probably hoping to protect himself, wished that his son Llewelyn would hold all judgments in abeyance. "Each truth," he wrote, "each lie, dies in unjudging love."

That I will not wish for you. Have your love and your judgment too.

If not wishes, how about aphorisms? Everyone can use an aphorism. I wish I could remember one, something especially Delphic or brilliant from "The Consolation of Philosophy," the *Bhagavad Gita,* the *Koran.*

Charlie Chan said: "Evidence like nose on anteater." Does that count?

Russians are better at such things. Once in my earshot Lillian Hellman observed: "A crazy person is crazy all the time."

I have frequently found that valuable, particularly when in the company of a crazy person who is, for the moment, lucid.

Confucius said: "Filial piety is the constant requirement of Heaven." That seems to me an excellent aphorism.

What would you say to purely tactical advice? Over the years I picked up several emotional maneuvers that might serve you well as contingency plans. When lonely, for example, read murder mysteries: I find them soothing. When angry, choose solitude. When lovesick, do push ups, run a mile or two, or step out with the boys. I don't know why that helps, but it does.

When bored, see the movie "Bringing Up Baby." When in despair, dress to the nines. I often wear a white shirt to work when I want to pit elegance against the fates. You might try that. (Do you own a white shirt?) When glum, call home.

Or should I present you with a parable? You've probably heard the ones about the good Samaritan and the Prodigal Son. No matter. Neither parable applies to you. You were born a good Samaritan and prodigality has never been one of your problems.

Frankly, I do not know a work of moral fiction that could improve your character, for it has always seemed to your mother and me (admittedly prejudiced but not blind) that your character never needed much improving. I have not known anyone more fair-minded, more considerate, more able to swallow disappointment. Not from me did you get these things. Why should I expect to give you something special now?

Unless, as in the old days, you would like a story. This is a true one (I can swear to it), about a father and a son in a playground 12 years ago, in the spring, around noon. The boy was five. He had a basketball, which he dribbled off his toes half the time, and which he kept shooting at the hoop—underhand, both hands, straining to reach the rim. The father sat on a bench and watched. The boy kept at it. Then some bigger boys sauntered over, snatched the ball away and shot around, leaving the five-year-old watching too.

Gearing up for the rescue, the father asked his son if he wanted him to retrieve the ball. The boy said, "No. I think I can handle it."

Which he did, simply by standing among the others patiently, occasionally catching the ball and passing it to one of them, until one of them eventually passed it to him. That's all there is to that story. The five-year-old continued to play ball, and his father sat in the sun.

Goodbye, my boy.

Roger Rosenblatt

Teachers

I am mighty glad that so many people in America are taking up the children work. I used to think there might be some chance of getting our government interested in it, but that was hoping too much. Being a ranchman and a farmer and also a child owner, I have often wished when one of my children got sick I could write or call some government expert and have him come look after them. Like I can do if one of my cows or pigs gets some disease.

If your fertilizer is not agreeing with your land the government will send a specialist, but if the food is not agreeing with baby, why we have to find out the matter ourselves, and lots of times parents mean well but they don't know much.

So I'm glad that you people are interested in children. Course they are a lot of trouble but we just don't seem to be smart enough to find something that would be less trouble that would replace them. It's not a bad idea whoever thought of doing something for the children. If it works out and you improve them, I will send you mine.

Will Rogers

Why Smoke?

It's a crazy world.

Most adults we know would love to look younger than they really are. While most young people are busy trying to look more adult.

This is one reason why many young people take up smoking.

Well, we wish they wouldn't.

For one thing, it doesn't work. A 15-year-old smoking a cigarette looks like nothing more or less than a 15-year-old smoking a cigarette.

Even though we're a tobacco company, we don't think young people should smoke. There is plenty of time later on to think about whether or not smoking is right for you.

Besides, when you think about it, being grown up is highly overrated. You have to go to work, pay taxes, wear normal clothes, and raise kids who grow up to be teenagers.

Why be in such a hurry?

R.J. Reynolds Tobacco Company
Promotional Poster

Volunteerism

Volunteers are like yachts.

No matter where they are, they arouse your curiosity. Who are they? Where do they come from? Why are they here?

They could stay moored where it's safe and still justify their being, but they choose to cut through the rough waters, ride out storms and take chances.

They have style. They're fiercely independent. If you have to ask how much they cost, you can't afford them.

Volunteers and yachts have a lot more in common these days. They're both part of an aristocratic era that is disappearing from the American scene. They're a luxury in a world that has become very practical.

Day by day, the number of volunteers decreases in this country as more and more of them equate their worth in terms of dollars and cents.

Three years ago I did a column on volunteers in an effort to point out they don't contribute to our civilization. They are our civilization, at least the only part worth talking about.

They are the only human beings on the face of this earth who reflect this nation's compassion, unselfishness, caring, patience, need, and just plain loving one another. Their very presence transcends politics, religion, ethnic background, marital status, sexism, even smokers vs. non-smokers.

Maybe, like the yacht, the volunteer was a luxury. And luxuries are often taken for granted.

One has to wonder. Did we, as a nation, remember to say to the volunteers, "Thank you for our symphony hall. Thank you for the six dialysis machines. Thank you for sitting up with a 16-year-old who overdosed and begged to die.

"Thank you for the hot chocolate at the scout meeting. Thanks for reading to the blind. Thanks for using your station wagon to transport a group of strangers to a ballgame.

"Thanks for knocking on doors in the rain. Thanks for hugging the winners of the Special Olympics. Thanks for pushing the wheelchair into the sun. Thanks for being."

Did the media stand behind them when they needed a boost? Did the professionals make it a point to tell them they did a good job? Did the recipients of their time and talent ever express their gratitude?

It frightens me, somehow, to imagine what the world will be like without them.

Erma Bombeck

Desiderata

Go placidly amid the noise, and haste, and remember what peace there may be in silence, as far as possible. Without surrender be on good terms with all persons. Speak your truth quietly and clearly; and listen to others, even the dull and ignorant; they too have their story. Avoid loud and aggressive persons, they are vexatious to the spirit. If you compare yourself with others, you may become vain and bitter; for always there will be greater and lesser persons than yourself. Enjoy your achievements as well as your plans. Keep interested in your own career, however humble; it is a real possession in the changing fortunes of time. Exercise caution in your business affairs; for the world is full of trickery. But let this not blind you to what virtue there is; many persons strive for high ideals; and everywhere life is full of heroism. Be yourself. Especially, do not feign affection. Neither be cynical about love; for in the face of all aridity and disenchantment it is perennial as the grass. Take kindly the counsel of the years, gracefully surrendering the things of youth. Nurture strength of spirit to shield you in sudden misfortune. But do not distress yourself with imaginings. Many fears are born of fatigue and loneliness. Beyond a wholesome discipline, be gentle with yourself. You are a child of the universe, no less than the trees and the stars; you have a right to be here. And whether or not it is clear to you, no doubt the universe is unfolding as it should.

Therefore be at peace with God, whatever you conceive Him to be, and whatever your labors and aspirations in the noisy confusion of life keep peace with your soul. With all its sham, drudgery, and broken dreams, it is still a beautiful world. Be careful. Strive to be happy.

What Is a Friend?

What is a friend? I will tell you. It is a person with whom you dare to be yourself. Your soul can be naked with him. He seems to ask of you to put on nothing, only to be what you are. He does not want you to be better or worse. When you are with him, you feel as a prisoner feels who has been declared innocent.

You do not have to be on your guard. You can say what you think, so long as it is genuinely you. He understands those contradictions in your nature that lead others to misjudge you. With him you breathe freely.

You can avow your little vanities and envies and hates and vicious sparks, your meannesses and absurdities and, in opening them up to him,

they are lost, dissolved on the white ocean of his loyalty. He understands. You do not have to be careful. You can abuse him, neglect him,
tolerate him. Best of all, you can keep still with him. It makes no matter.

He is like fire that purges to the bone. He understands. You can weep
with him, sin with him, laugh with him, pray with him. Through it
all—and underneath—he sees, knows, and loves you.

A friend? What is a friend? Just one, I repeat, with whom you dare to
be yourself.

C. Raymond Beran

Just for Today

- Just for today I will try to live through this day only, and not set
  far-reaching goals to try to overcome all my problems at once.
- Just for today I will try to be happy. Abraham Lincoln said, "Most
  folks are about as happy as they make up their minds to be." He was
  right. I will not dwell on thoughts that depress me.
- Just for today I will adjust myself to what is. I will face reality. I will
  try to change those things that I can change and accept those things I
  cannot change.
- Just for today, I will try to improve my mind. I will not be a mental
  loafer. I will force myself to read something that requires an effort.
- Just for today I will do a good deed for somebody—without letting
  him know it.
- Just for today I will do something positive to improve my health. And
  I will force myself to exercise—even if it's only walking around the
  block, or using the stairs instead of the elevator.
- Just for today I will be totally honest. If someone asks me something I
  don't know, I will not try to bluff; I'll simply say, "I don't know."
- Just for today I'll do something I've been putting off for a long time.
- Just for today, before I speak I will ask myself, "Is it true? Is it kind?"
  And if the answer to either of those questions is negative, I won't say
  it.
- Just for today I will make a conscious effort to be agreeable, I will look
  as well as I can, dress becomingly, talk softly, act courteously, and not
  interrupt when someone else is talking.
- Just for today I will be unafraid. I will gather the courage to do what is
  right and take the responsibility for my own actions.

Ann Landers

Today's the Day To Give Thanks

How's your health? Not so good? Well, thank God you've lived this
long. A lot of people haven't. You're hurting, more. (Have you ever
visited a veterans' hospital? Or a rehabilitation clinic for crippled children?)

If you awakened this morning and were able to hear the birds sing, use
your vocal cords to utter human sounds, walk to the breakfast table on

'o good legs and read the newspaper with two good eyes, praise the Lord! A lot of people couldn't.

How's your pocketbook? Thin. Well, most of the world is a lot poorer. No pensions. No welfare. No food stamps. No Social Security. In fact, one-third of the people in the world will go to bed hungry tonight.

Are you lonely? The way to have a friend is to be one. If nobody calls you, call someone. Go out of your way to do something nice for somebody. It's a sure cure for the blues.

Are you concerned about your country's future? Hooray! Our system has been saved by such concern. Concern for fair play under the law. Your country may not be a rose garden, but it also is not a patch of weeds.

Freedom rings! Look and listen. You can still worship at the church of your choice, cast a secret ballot, and even criticize your government without fearing a knock on the head or a knock on the door at midnight. And if you want to live under a different system, you are free to go.

As a final thought, I'll repeat my Thanksgiving Prayer; perhaps you will want to use it at your table today:

O, heavenly Father: We thank thee for food and remember the
    hungry.
We thank thee for health and remember the sick.
We thank thee for friends and remember the friendless.
We thank thee for freedom and remember the enslaved.
May these remembrances stir us to service.
That thy gifts to us may be used for others. Amen.

Ann Landers

You see things; and you say, "Why?" But I dream things that never were; and I say, "Why not?"

G.B. Shaw

No man is an island, entire of itself; every man is a piece of the continent, a part of the main; if a clod be washed away by the sea, Europe is the less, as well as if a promontory were, as well as if a manor of thy friends, or of thine own were; any man's death diminishes me, because I am involved in mankind; and therefore never send to know for whom the bell tolls; it tolls for thee.

John Donne

An American

I have befouled the waters and polluted the air of a magnificent land.
But I have made it safe from disease.

I have flown through the sky faster than the sun.
But I have idled in streets made ugly with traffic.

60

I have littered the land with garbage,
But I have built upon it a hundred million homes.

I have divided schools with my prejudice,
But I have sent armies to unite them.

I have beaten down my enemies with clubs,
But I have built courtrooms to keep them free.

I have built the bomb to destroy the world,
But I have used it to light a light.

I have outraged my brothers in alleys of ghettos,
But I have transplanted a human heart.

I have scribbled out filth and pornography,
But I have elevated the philosophy of man.

I have watched children starve from my golden towers,
But I have fed half of the world.

I was raised in a grotesque slum,
But I am surfeited by the silver spoon of opulence.

I live in the greatest country in the world and the greatest time in history,
But I scorn the ground I stand upon.

I am ashamed,
But I am proud.

I am an American.

Anonymous

A Teacher

No printed word
Nor spoken plea,
Can teach young minds
What they should be;
Nor all the books
On all the shelves—
But what the teachers
are themselves.

H. Ginnott

I Am a Child

I am a child,
All the world waits for my coming
All the world watches with interest
To see what I shall become.
The future hangs in the balance
For what I am,
The world of tomorrow will be.

I am a child,
I have come into your world
About which I know nothing,
Why I came I know not.
How I came I know not.
I am curious.
I am interested.
I am a child,
You hold in your hand my destiny
You determine, largely,
Whether I shall succeed or fail,
Give me, I pray you,
Those things that make for happiness.
Train me, I beg you,
That I may be a blessing to the world.

Anonymous

Life

Don't ever try to understand everything—some things will just never
make sense.
Don't ever be reluctant to show your feelings—
When you're happy, give in to it!
When you're not, live with it.
Don't ever be afraid to try to make things better—
You might be surprised at the results.
Don't ever take the weight of the world on your shoulders.
Don't ever feel threatened by the future—take life one day at a time.
Don't ever feel guilty about the past—what's done is done. Learn from
any mistakes you might have made.
Don't ever feel that you are alone . . . there is always somebody there for
you to reach out to.
Don't ever feel that you cannot achieve so many of the things you can
imagine—imagine that! It's not as hard as it seems
Don't ever stop believing, don't ever stop dreaming your dreams.

Norman Vincent Peale

The Bridge Builder

An old man, going a lone highway,
Came at the evening, cold and gray
To a chasm, vast and deep and wide,
Through which was flowing a sullen tide.
The old man crossed in the twilight dim—
That sullen stream had no fears for him;
But he turned, when he reached the other side,
And built a bridge to span the tide.

"Old man," said a fellow pilgrim near,
"You are wasting strength in building here.
Your journey will end with the ending day;
You never again must pass this way.
You have crossed the chasm, deep and wide,
Why build you the bridge at the eventide?"

The builder lifted his old gray head.
"Good friend, in the path I have come," he said,
"There followeth after me today
A youth whose feet must pass this way.
This chasm that has been naught to me
To that fair-haired youth may a pitfall be.
He, too, must cross in the twilight dim;
Good friend, I am building the bridge for him."

Will Allen Dromgoole

Listen, World!

God, all night long I miss him.
Lying half asleep—my conscious memory lost.
I wonder if he tossed the blankets off.
Or if the rain is blowing on his sill.
Or if he's ill—my baby.
And often waking, I find myself beside his bed,
Stopping to kiss the little tousled head that is no longer there.
I stand and stare with streaming eyes
At that smooth pillow and unruffled spread.
Remembering slowly, that my son is dead.
All day long I listen for his step.
His whistle and his sweet, uncertain song.
I listen until the silence tightens round my throat.
Oh God, you know I'd give my life to hear his voice again.
To feel, once more, the touch of his young, eager hand.
To stand and watch him play,
And feel the pride leap in me like a flame.
I'd give my life, I say—and yet I wouldn't
I must stay right here and do my job, till I have earned the right to go away.
The past has passed.
I loved him—yes, But love is not a toy
To satisfy one's private price and joy.
No—love's a part of that eternal plan
By which God manifests himself to man.
And we who love must also dare to keep the faith
When those we love are lost,
Lest weaker spirits, watching, should cry out that love's not worth the cost.

And so, my Father, take my grief today as tribute to the glory you sent away.
I lay my little son within your arms, safe now, forever, from the hurt and harm
He would have known, had he lived.
I give him up, I drink the bitter cup reserved for those who dare to love and lose.
Forgive our fears!
There is a nobler duty facing us than tears.
It is our proud and shining mission to express
Love's rare, abiding pride and loveliness.
We only, who have lost, can know that love is worth
Whatever it may cost.

Anonymous

Poring Over a Bad Love Affair

I first met her in high school. She was older than I, and exciting. She'd been around. My parents warned me to have nothing to do with her. They claimed no good could come from our relationship.

But I kept meeting her on the sly. She was so sophisticated and worldly. It made me feel grown up just being with her. It was fun to take her to a party in those days. She was almost always the center of attention.

We began seeing more of each other after I started college. When I got a place of my own, she was a frequent guest. It wasn't long before she moved in. It may have been common-law, but it was heartbreaking for my parents. I kept reminding myself I wasn't a kid any more. Besides, it was legal.

We lived together right through college and into my early days in business. I seldom went anywhere without her, but I wasn't blind. I knew she was unfaithful to me. What's worse, I didn't care. As long as she was there for me when I needed her (and she always was) it didn't matter.

The longer we lived together, the more attached I became to her. But it wasn't mutual. She began to delight in making me look foolish in front of my friends. But still I couldn't give her up.

It became a love/hate relationship. I figured out that her glamour was nothing more than a cheap mask to hide her spite and cynicism. I could no longer see her beauty after I came to know her true character.

But old habits are hard to break. We had invested many years in each other. Even though my relationship with her made me lose a little respect for myself, she had become the center of my life. We didn't go anywhere. We didn't do anything. We didn't have friends over. It was just the two of us. I became deeply depressed and knew that she was largely responsible for my misery. I finally told her I was leaving for good. It took a lot of guts but I left.

I still see her around. She's as beautiful as when we met. I still miss her now and then. I'm not boasting when I say she'd take me back in a minute. But by the grace of God, I will never take up with her again.

If you see her give her my regards. I don't hate her. I just loved her too much. Chances are you know her family. The name is Alcohol.

Ann Landers

A Campus Thought

People who go to college are incredible. We live away from home. We go to classes. We read and absorb and are tested on heavy amounts of various materials. We sleep very little. We drink. We cough and keep smoking.

Someone's always sick. Someone's always complaining.

We become attached to close friends. We smother each other. We lean too much. We talk too much. We think way too much. We feel too much. We think often of the past and want to be back there. We know we cannot go. We all have our separate lives and families, backgrounds and pasts.

We live totally different from how we used to live. We are frustrated and although sometimes we want to give up, we never stop trying. We disregard health. We eat awful food. We are forced to think about the future. We are scared and confused.

We reach out for things but don't find them. We try to sort out our minds, which are filled with studies, worries, problems, memories, emotions—powerful feelings. We wander the hall looking for happiness. We wonder where we fit in. We fall and get back up.

We hurt—a lot. We keep on going, tough, because above all else, we never stop learning, growing, changing, and most importantly, dreaming.

Dreams keep us going. And they always will. All we can do about that is thank God that we have something to hold on to.

Lynn Fulginiti

Act To Stop Teen Suicide

I am a high school student whose friend committed suicide 2 1/2 years ago. This letter is in response to two articles appearing in the past two weeks. On Thursday, June 5, we learned that another teenager had killed himself. A week later, on Wednesday, June 11, the State Assembly passed a bill that would assist local communities in dealing with the problems of teenage suicide. This legislation still needs the approval of the State Senate and Governor Cuomo.

How very unfortunate that my peers and I have to wait until money is, if ever, officially allocated before suicide prevention programs are put into place. We should be calling upon our junior and senior high schools to take a more personal approach toward our education and to approach this topic.

It doesn't take a whole lot of money for a school counselor, sensitive teacher, or guest speaker to discuss with students feelings about suicide, making them aware of the warning signals of depression and suicidal behavior; to teach them what to do if they spot these signs and to introduce them to support systems already available outside school. Such methods are already being used by schools covering alcoholism and drug abuse, family life, and "sex education." People must stop treating suicide as a taboo subject.

The state money could then be used to expand upon this base, for example, by involving parents and educators in more detailed workshops. What is most important is that they learn the most effective ways in which to express their concern now. Without concerned and caring people behind it, no amount of money is going to prevent anyone from taking his or her life.

Even the most conservative facts speak for themselves. Adolescent suicide is an epidemic, and for each completed suicide, there are 10 others seriously contemplating killing themselves. Must more lives be wasted before something is done?

Lynn Mulheron

Our Country

There is a new spirit abroad in the land.
The old days of grab and greed are gone.
We're beginning to think of what we owe the other fellow.
Not just what we're compelled to give him.
The time is coming when we shalln't be able to fill our bellies in comfort—while others shiver in the cold.
We shalln't be able to kneel and thank God for blessings before our shining altar, while men anywhere are kneeling in either physical or spiritual subjection
And God willing—we'll live to see that day.

Sir Arthur Conan Doyle

LaMancha

Call nothing your own—except your soul
Love not what you are—but only what you could become.
Don't pursue pleasures—because you might have the misfortune of overtaking them.
Look always forward—
Be just to all men—
And courteous to all women—
Live always in the vision for whom great things are done.

Don Miguel Cervantes

Oh, my friend—I have lived almost 50 years and I have seen life as it is—pain, misery, hunger, cruelty beyond belief—and I have heard the singing from the taverns and the moans from the bundles of filth in the streets.

I've been a soldier and I've seen my comrades fall in battle—or die more slowly under the lash in Africa. I've held them in my arms at the FINAL MOMENT—these were men who saw life as it is and yet they died despairing—no glory, no gallant last word—only their eyes filled with confusion, whimpering the question: "WHY?" And I don't think they asked why they were dying—but rather, why they had lived.

And life itself seems lunatic—who knows where madness lies. Perhaps too much sanity may be madness. To seek treasure where there is only trash—perhaps to be practical is madness—and maddest of all is to see life as it is and not as IT OUGHT TO BE.

Don Miguel Cervantes

There are those, I know, who will reply that the liberation of humanity, the freedom of man and mind, is nothing but a dream . . . they are right—it is the American Dream.

A. MacLeish

What has after maintained the Human Race on this old globe—despite all the calamities of nature and all the tragic failing of mankind, if not faith in new possibilities and courage to advocate them.

Jane Addams

What kind of man would live where there is no daring? I don't believe in foolish chances, but nothing can be accomplished without taking any chance at all.

C. Lindbergh

A leader is best
When people barely know he exists.
Not so good when people obey and acclaim him,
Worse when they despise him.
"Fail to honor people, They fail to honor you";
But of a good leader, who talks little,
When his work is done, his aim fulfilled,
They will say, "We did this ourselves."

Lao-Tse

Dear Teacher:
I am a survivor of a concentration camp. My eyes saw what no one should ever witness:
Gas chambers built by learned engineers,
Children poisoned by educated physicians,
Infants killed by trained nurses,
Women and babies burned and shot by college and high school graduates.
It is this that I am suspicious of "Education."
My request is a simple one. Teach your children the basics but more importantly—help them to become "human." Reading, writing, and math are important, but only if they serve to make our children more humane.

H. Ginott

Our greatest natural resource is the minds of our children.

W. Disney

Throughout the centuries there were men who took first steps down new roads armed with nothing but their own vision.

A. Rand

American Indian Prayer
Red Cloud Indian School, Pine Ridge, S.Dak.
(Used by permission)

O great Spirit, whose voice I hear in the winds, and whose breath gives life to all the world, hear me!
I am small and weak; I need your strength and wisdom.
Let me walk in beauty, and make my eyes ever behold the red and purple sunset.
Make my hands respect the things you have made and my ears sharp to hear your voice.
Make me wise so that I may understand the things you have taught my people.
Let me learn the lessons you have hidden in every leaf and rock.
I seek strength, not to be greater than my friend, but to fight my greatest enemy—myself.
Make me always ready to come to you with clean hands and straight eyes.
So when life fades, as the fading sunset, may my spirit come to you without shame.

Quotable Quotes

Never tell a young person that anything cannot be done. God may have been waiting for centuries for somebody ignorant enough of the impossible to do that very thing.

John Andrew Holmes

You are what you are when nobody is looking.

Ann Landers

What I do today is important because I am exchanging a day of my life for it.

Hugh Mulligan

Pain is inevitable, Suffering is optional.

Bonnie Bogdanoff

A man never stands so straight as when he stoops to help a boy.

Fr. Flanagan

We ought to be interested in the future, for that is where we are going to spend the rest of our lives.

Thomas Jefferson

. . . I belong here completely and utterly. I'm home. The world has caught up with me and surpassed me. Ninety years ago I was a freak—now I'm an amateur.

H.G. Wells

Always aim for achievement and forget about success.

Helen Hayes

. . . It's time for a new generation of leadership, to cope with new problems and new opportunities. For there is a new world to be won.

John F. Kennedy

A leader, by definition, is a person with a following and a cause.

Harry S Truman

You know what makes leadership? It is the ability to get men to do what they don't want to do, and like it.

Harry S Truman

If I could reach up
and hold a star
for each time
you made me smile,
an entire evening's sky
would be in
the palm of my hand.

Rowland Hoskins

My friend, if I could give you one thing
I would give you the ability to see yourself
As others see you . . .
Then you would realize what a truly special
person you are.

Barb B. Howland

. . . No matter what accomplishment you make—somebody helps us.
Althea Gibson

. . . I think the true discovery of America is before us. I think the true fulfillment of our spirit, of our people, of our mighty and immortal land is yet to come.

Thomas Wolfe

. . . Bring me men
To match my mountains.
Bring me one
To match my plains
Men with empires
In their purpose
Ane new eras
In their brains.

Sam Foss

We are here to add
what we can to life,
not get what we can
from it.

William Ossler

If your mind can conceive it
and your heart can believe it
then you can achieve it.

Jesse Jackson

Truth

Why shouldn't truth be stranger than fiction? Fiction, after all, has to
make sense.

Mark Twain

I never give them hell, I just tell and they think it's hell.

Harry S Truman

Truth or tact? You have to choose. Most times they are not compatible.

Eddie Cantor

Truth—what we think it is at any given moment of time.

Luigi Pirandello

Work

A man's work is his dilemma: his job is his bondage, but it also gives him
a fair share of his identity and keeps him from being a bystander in
somebody else's world.

Melvin Maddocks

Nothing is really work unless you would rather be doing something else.

James M. Barrie

We work to become, not to acquire.

Elbert Hubbard

Work is what you do so that some time you won't have to do it any more.

Alfred Poigar

Whenever two people meet there are really six people present. There is each man as he sees himself, each man as the other person sees him, and each man as he really is.

William James

Pessimism

A pessimist is a man who looks both ways before crossing a one-way street.

Laurence J. Peter

Pessimist: One who, when he has the choice of two evils, chooses both.

Oscar Wilde

There is no sadder sight than a young pessimist.

Mark Twain

The difference between bad luck and good luck is the difference in our attitude toward circumstances and events. The human mind sometimes converts the greatest blessings into the most sordid evils. But the spiritual minded person takes whatever comes and at once seeks the blessing contained therein. By looking, we always locate what we seek.

Adelaide Hensley

The sure way to miss success is to miss the opportunity.

Victor Chasies

The gates of opportunity and advancement swing on these four hinges: initiative, industry, insight, and integrity.

William Arthur Ward

Luck

Luck may win a few deals, but in the long run it is the better player who scores the highest. Chance may throw a fortune into anyone's lap, but what is termed luck usually is the fruit of shrewdness and persistency.

Baltasar Gracian

I'm a great believer in luck, and I find the harder I work the more I have of it.

Thomas Jefferson

Faith

What I admire in Columbus is not his having discovered a world, but his having gone to search for it on the faith of an opinion.

A. Robert Turgot

Treat the other man's faith gently, it is all he has to believe with.

Henry S. Haskins

Faith—an illogical belief in the occurrence of the improbable.

H.L. Mencken

Life is doubt, and faith without doubt is nothing but death.

Miguel de Unamuno

Failure

In the game of life it's a good idea to have a few early losses, which relieves you of the pressure of trying to maintain an undefeated season.

Bill Vaughan

There is no failure except in no longer trying.

Elbert Laing

You never know where bottom is until you plumb for it.

Frederick Laing

Good people are good because they've come to wisdom through failure.

William Saroyan

Education

Perhaps the most valuable result of all education is the ability to make yourself do the thing you have to do, when it ought to be done, whether you like it or not.

Thomas Henry Huxley

A school should not be a preparation for life. A school should be life.

Elbert Hubbard

The great end of education is to discipline rather than to furnish the mind, to train it to the use of its own powers, rather than fill it with the accumulation of others.

Tryon Edwards

Education today, more than ever before, must see clearly the dual objectives: education for living and educating for making a living.

James Mason Wood

Death

There is no cure for birth or death save to enjoy the interval.

George Santayana

The reports of my death are greatly exaggerated.

Mark Twain

I'm not afraid to die. I just don't want to be there when it happens.

Woody Allen

The more complex one's life is, the more . . . one's creative capacities are fulfilled, the less one fears death . . . people are not afraid of death per se, but of the incompleteness of their lives.

Lis Marburg Goodman

Courage

One man with courage makes a majority.

Andrew Jackson

Valor lies just halfway between rashness and cowardice.

Don Miguel Cervantes

Courage is a good word. It has a ring. It is a substance that other people, who have none, urge you to have when all is lost.

Jim Bishop

Courage, it would seem, is nothing less than the power to overcome danger, misfortune, fear, injustice, while continuing to affirm inwardly that life with all its sorrows and good is meaningful even if in a sense beyond our understanding, and that there is always tomorrow.

Dorothy Thompson

Bravery is being the only one who knows you're afraid.

Franklin P. Jones

Courage is grace under pressure.

Ernest Hemingway

Ability

Real success is not an outward show but an inward feeling. It begins inside, and probably its first inkling is the feeling, even the knowledge, that one is worthwhile. That's quite a discovery. Regardless of how the world may value us, there is no fooling the inner Bureau of Standards.

Howard J. Whitman

To Be Nobody But Yourself

to be nobody but yourself
in a world which is doing
its best day and night to
make you everybody else
means to fight the hardest
battle which any
human being can
fight and never
stop fighting.

e. e. cummings

To every man his chance
to every man regardless of birth
his shining golden opportunity—
to every man his right to live
to work, to be himself
and to become whatever thing
his manhood and his wisdom
can combine to make him.
This . . . is the promise of America.

Thomas Wolfe

It is easy enough to tell the poor to accept their poverty as God's will when you yourself have warm clothes and plenty of food and medical care and a roof over your head and no worry about the rent. But if you want them to believe you, try to share some of their poverty and see if you can accept it as God's will yourself!

Thomas Merton

If there is right in the soul,
There will be beauty in the person;
If there is beauty in the person,
There will be harmony in the home;
If there is harmony in the home,
There will be order in the nation;
If there is order in the nation,
There will be peace in the world.

Chinese Proverb

It is better to light one candle than to curse the darkness.

Christopher Motto

Hope looks for the good in people instead of harping on the worst.

Hope opens doors where despair closes them.

Hope discovers what can be done instead of grumbling about what cannot . . . .

Hope "lights a candle" instead of "cursing the darkness."

Hope regards problems, small or large, as opportunities.

Hope cherishes no illusions, nor does it yield to cynicism.

Hope sets big goals and is not frustrated by repeated difficulties or setbacks.

Hope puts up with modest gains, realizing that "the longest journey starts with one step."

Hope accepts misunderstandings as the price for serving the greater good of others.

Hope is a good loser because it has the divine assurance of final victory.

James Keller

Difficult things to do:

To break a bad habit,
To love an enemy,
To think logically,
To admit ignorance,
To withhold judgment,
To grow old gracefully,
To persevere without haste,
To wait without impatience,
To suffer without complaint,
To know when to keep silent,
To be indifferent to ridicule,
To concentrate in the midst of strife,
To endure hatred without resentment,
To fraternize without losing individuality,
To serve without compensation, commendation, recognition.

Anonymous

A Short Course in Thinking

1. Be honest with yourself. Avoid the temptation to self-delusion.
2. Confront problems; don't evade them. Growth comes through facing reality.
3. Widen your interests. Stretch your mind by reading, conversation, listening.
4. Write out the problem. Positive action depends on clear thinking. Writing helps.
5. Keep first things first. Focus on the main issue; don't be confused by non-essentials.

6. Don't oversimplify. If a problem is serious enough to bother you, it's worth pondering.
7. Get beyond fault finding. People know what's wrong. They want to know what to do about it.
8. Keep an open mind. The best solution may not be your solution.
9. Retain your sense of humor. Humor can reduce prejudice and put things in perspective.
10. Develop insight. Listen for what the other person means, not merely what he says.
11. Focus on the positive. Emphasize points of agreement while admitting differences.

Christopher News

The Cop Who Spreads Sunshine

For six years William Sample, a 40-year-old police officer, had been assigned to protective duty at St. Christopher's Hospital for Children in Philadelphia. Among the patients were a large number of chronically or terminally ill children, suffering from such afflictions as cancer, cystic fibrosis, and kidney disease. Over the years, Sample came to know many of the children and, as well, families who had been drained financially and emotionally. He wished constantly that he could do something to ease their suffering.

Then, one evening in October 1976, a dream of an idea occurred to him. "Every one of these kids must have some special wish," he said to his fiancee, Helene, who was assistant personnel manager at the hospital. "I can't do anything to make them physically better. But maybe I can make some of their dreams come true."

Helene let the idea seep in for a minute. "Let's do it," she said.

They called nine people, men and women who cared greatly about children, to a meeting. Bill's enthusiasm was contagious, and soon the others eagerly offered to join the project. What to call it? "How about 'Sunshine'?" someone suggested. "Because we'll be putting a little sunshine into children's lives." Applause. Agreement.

"That's it, then," Bill said. "The Sunshine Foundation."

In January 1977, Sunshine cast its first ray when the cheerful, round-faced cop—scarcely anybody's idea of a Fairy Godmother—found five-year-old Bobby, who was dying of leukemia, sitting in St. Christopher's waiting room with his parents. Bill asked Bobby what he would like to do or have above anything else. Bobby said he didn't know, but a nurse had told Bill that the boy yearned to play in the snow.

"How about a weekend at a resort hotel in the Pocono Mountains?" he asked. "Everybody goes. You, your sister and brother, your folks. Sound good?"

Bobby nodded. Bill looked at the parents, and they nodded too. But the expressions on their faces told him that they weren't sure what they were encountering.

At this point Sunshine was still penniless, so Bill sent the Pocono hotel a personal check to cover the reservation for Bobby and his family. Bill, Helene, and several other Sunshine volunteers decided to go, too. "We didn't want to be nosy," Bill explains. "But we wanted to see if we were doing the right thing. Was Sunshine worthwhile? Did it matter?"

It mattered. "Bobby rode the snowmobile and toboggan, and even skied," Bill recalls. "His father said he showed more energy than he had in a year. In the excitement of enjoying himself, he grew less aware of his pain. For a few days the horror in the lives of this family retreated a little."

Several days later Bobby's mother telephoned Bill: "We'll never forget the weekend, never forget what you did for Bobby, never forget you."

That weekend determined the new course of Bill's life. But making dreams come true costs money, and none of the Sunshiners had a feasible fund raising idea. They had tried bingo, with Bill borrowing $2,300 from a bank to rent a hall and provide prizes. Bill and his Sunshiners, however, could not compete with Philadelphia's professionally run bingo tournaments.

By May 1977, Bill had personally borrowed $4,500 on behalf of Sunshine. Although an unquenchable optimist, he could see his wonderful idea winding up as a pipe dream.

Then, when his gloom was deepest, publicity by a Philadelphia newspaper columnist and Bill's appearances on local radio shows began attracting a rising flow of small donations. By 1978, Sunshine had some 30 volunteers. They sold raffle tickets, cookbooks, and cakes; they ran dances, flea markets, and fashion shows.

Soon there was enough for Bill to rent an apartment near the beach at Ocean City, N.J. That summer 10 families spent a week each at the beach, and for the first time in their lives some sick kids played in the sand and sat on the shore with the sea lapping at their legs.

In 1978, the Commonwealth of Pennsylvania gave the Sunshine Foundation the first of three annual $25,000 grants. Vastly encouraged, Bill enlisted staff members at St. Christopher's and Children's Hospital in the search for unfulfilled dreams, and sent letters to children's hospitals in every other major American city. Responses came from all over the country, and they have been coming in increasing numbers each year since.

A girl in Oregon wants a pony. A little boy in Illinois dreams of sitting on the deck of a houseboat as it eases down the Mississippi. An Indiana girl would love to touch a California redwood.

No wish has ever been denied. An Oklahoma girl yearned to visit relatives in California, but was too sick to travel. So Sunshine flew the California family to Oklahoma. A computer went to a New Jersey boy who was confined to a wheelchair and unable to speak. He now uses the computer to "talk" with his family.

Sometimes a Sunshine Foundation effort to grant a wish inspires a community response. A couple in West Virginia wrote that their daughter, who had leukemia, and who shared with them the only bedroom in their small cottage, wanted a room of her own more than anything else. Sunshine had a local building supply company deliver needed materials—and friends and neighbors helped the girl's father build the additional room.

Many parents are understandably reluctant to ask for "charity"—or simply don't believe Sunshine is for real. In these instances Sunshine frequently learns of the child's plight from someone connected with the family.

A friend wrote about 13-year-old Sam, who had a rare malignancy of the spine and was not given much hope for recovery. His great wish was to sit in the stands at the 1982 Super Bowl game in Pontiac, Mich.

Sunshine telephoned the family and told the mother that her son's dream would be fulfilled. "I don't really believe this is happening," she exclaimed.

It was the end of December, and the Super Bowl game would be played on January 24. The stadium was sold out. Sunshine telephoned the executive offices of the Philadelphia Eagles and requested, with an explanation, five tickets from the team's allotment. The answer was a quick yes.

The news was telephoned to Sam. "Am I really going?" he asked, breaking into tears, "I can't believe it."

The Super Bowl game thrilled Sam and so did the autograph given him by victorious San Francisco quarterback Joe Montana. The family wrote, "Words are sometimes hard to find when you are trying to say thank you for something so priceless as love and kindness."

Occasionally, physicians appeal to Sunshine. An Ohio doctor wrote about his patient Gary, a 12-year-old with congenital heart disease. "He has been ill all his life and I doubt that he will live another year. At present, he can hardly walk 50 yards without becoming short of breath and exhausted. Like all children, he dreams of going to Disney World. But his parents cannot afford it. They live in near poverty."

Sunshine made the necessary arrangements for Gary's trip and, once again, dream became reality.

Upon the family's return from Disney World, the doctor reported: "A truly miraculous thing has happened. I don't have any way medically to explain it. Gary made a tremendous gain in physical endurance and was able to navigate easily over his five-day stay in Florida. His breathing was unlabored all during the trip. I can only assume the climate was responsible for his well-being. His father is going back to Florida to look for a job. This may be one case in which the Sunshine Foundation has been able to prolong life as well as make a child's dream come true."

The family did move to Florida and later told the doctor Gary was doing very well.

Another doctor wrote to Sunshine about Suzanne, who had "severe burn scars on her face, scalp, and body. She has had 20 hospitalizations with numerous surgeries for plastic repairs. She will survive, but will be disfigured."

The mother, divorced and living on a bare survival income, had no telephone. Pride prevented her from answering several Sunshine letters. The doctor finally persuaded her to reply.

She told the Samples, "Suzanne and I have done a lot of talking. The one thing she wants is a Barbie doll's remote-control car. She also wants a watch. Anything you can do to help her have a nice Christmas would be appreciated."

With the Foundation short of cash as usual, two Sunshine women borrowed Sample's credit card to go shopping. On Christmas Eve, Bill and a volunteer dressed as Santa packed up the gifts—including Barbie and Ken dolls and an array of outfits for both, the Barbie car, and the watch, and drove to Suzanne's apartment. She stared at them in astonishment. "Santa, why haven't you been here before?" she asked. After joyously opening her presents, Suzanne led the visitors into the kitchen. "Here, Santa," she said, "I made some cookies for you."

Later, the two men drove to Bill's house, savoring the best Christmas Eve they had ever spent.

To Sunshine, every request is urgent. Several children have died before their dreams could be fulfilled, and others soon after.

In November 1981, one mother wrote: "It breaks my heart to tell you that on October 2 we lost Brian to his disease. We are sending you a $50 check. Brian had a yard sale and raised the money himself. He wanted it to go to you because you gave him one of the most important things of his life—not only the trip to Florida but a new view of people who give so unselfishly of themselves. He never stopped talking about the trip."

So far Sunshine has fulfilled 600 dreams. The foundation headquarters has grown from Bill's briefcase to three rooms above a Philadelphia hardware store. There, four dedicated young women answer the mail and make necessary arrangements. Upon request, they send applications, which include a question about family income, to parents of very sick children. The return of a completed application is followed by a letter to the child's physician, requesting the diagnosis, prognosis, and restrictions, if any, on the child's ability to travel.

The Foundation has no wealthy or corporate supporters who can be counted on for regular contributions, and Bill remains a full-time cop. Although he has enough service time to retire, he can't afford to.

"Sunshine is still mostly a nickel and dime operation," he says. "Many times we've been desperate for money to give a child his or her wish. But somehow, in the next day or two, the mails have always brought us the money we needed.

"You know," he says, his strong voice dropping to a whisper, "sometimes I have the feeling that the kids whose dreams we've fulfilled and who have since died are seeing to it that we have what we need to help children who need us today."

Joseph P. Blank

Send Someone a Smile

One day shortly after my third child was born, I received a note from another young mother, a friend of mine who lived just three blocks from me. We hadn't seen each other all winter.

"Hi, friend," she wrote, "I think of you often. Someday we'll have time to spend together like in the old days. Keep plugging. I know you're a super mother. See you soon, I hope."

It was signed: "Your friend on hold, Sue Ann."

The few words lifted my spirits and added a soothing ointment of love to a hectic day. I remember thinking, "Thanks, Sue Ann. I needed that."

The next day was my errand day, because my husband was home to tend the children. I decided to visit a card shop a few miles away that was having a sale. I wasn't in a good mood. The baby had a cold, and I was in a hurry.

Instead of reacting to my brusqueness, the saleswoman was extremely courteous and helpful. Noticing that her name tag read Janet Sullivan, I asked the woman if she was the store owner. "Oh, no," she said. "I'm just one of the employees, but I love it here." I left the shop feeling more able to cope.

On the way home, I thought, I really ought to write a note to the owner of that shop and tell her what a good employee Janet Sullivan is. But, of course, there isn't time.

When I arrived home, however, things seemed peaceful. On my desk I saw my friend Sue Ann's note. If she had the time to lift my spirits, why, I had time to help cheer others.

"Dear Store Owner," I wrote, "It was a hectic morning and I came into your shop with a chip on my shoulder. But Janet Sullivan was pleasant, extremely helpful, and she did not let my uptight mood affect her kindness to me. Thank you for hiring such a lovely lady and for making my day better." I signed the note, "A satisfied customer."

Next I wrote to Janet Sullivan. It all took only a few minutes, but the rest of my day seemed to glide by more smoothly than usual. I decided I would write notes more often when I ran into people who were doing a good job.

That Monday my six-year-old came home from school with a clever puppet and several other delightful learning tools. For quite a while, I had been impressed with the good job Meagan's teacher was doing, yet I had never told her.

Why not? I thought, as I pulled out another sheet of stationery.

"Dear Miss Patrick," I began. "Your clever ideas make learning fun. My daughter loves school. You seem to have time for the individual child, and I frankly don't know how you do it. I'm so happy that there are dedicated teachers like you who have talent and love for their jobs. Thanks for giving my little girl a good start and a good attitude toward learning.

"Sincerely, A Happy Mom."

I decided not to sign the note. I didn't want Miss Patrick to think I was trying to help my daughter to be better-liked.

When I went out to mail Miss Patrick's note, I noticed a neighbor checking his mailbox. Mr. Williams' head drooped and his pace seemed slower as he shuffled back to his house empty-handed. I hurried back into my own house because I could hear my baby crying, but I couldn't get Mr. Williams off my mind. It wasn't a check he was waiting for; he was quite well-to-do. He was probably looking for some love in his mailbox.

While Meagan drew a picture of a mailbox with a smile in it and Tami drew a rainbow, I wrote a little note. "We are your secret admirers," it began. We added a favorite story and a poem. "Expect to hear from us often," I wrote on the envelope.

The next day my children and I watched Mr. Williams take out his mail and open the envelope right in the driveway. Even at a distance, we could see he was smiling.

My mind began reeling when I thought of all the people who could use smiles in their mailboxes. What about the 15-year-old Down's Syndrome girl near my parents whose birthday was coming up? The endless people I didn't even know who still believe in courtesy and in doing a good job? Even on busy days I could find the time to write at least one note.

Hundreds of notes later, I have made two discoveries:

1. Notes don't need to be long. When my neighbors, the Linthrops, moved, I heard several other neighbors comment on how much they missed them. My note from our street was extremely short.

"Dear Linthrops," I wrote. "When you moved, you took some sunshine with you. People here miss your smiles and happy voices. Please come back to visit. Your friends on Cherry Lane."

2. Anonymous notes leave others free of obligation. It is difficult for people to accept compliments or help, and anonymous notes alleviate any embarrassment or feelings that they must acknowledge or reciprocate in any way.

At first, I wanted credit for the notes. But, now, writing them in secret adds a sense of adventure. It's more fun. I once overheard talk of the Phantom Note Lady. They were discussing me, but they didn't know, and I wasn't telling.

Perhaps I will never have the means and the time to help others in magnificent ways, even after our children are grown. But right now it is satisfying to know that I am helping to lift spirits in small ways. I have found that it is easy to find the time to write letters of praise, love, and appreciation. And as a side effect, I find myself looking at my own circumstances in a much more positive light. But then, happiness usually is a side effect.

Ann Bateman

The Miracle of May Lemke's Love

The Milwaukee County General Hospital had a serious problem: a six-month-old infant named Leslie. Mentally retarded and without eyes, the baby also had cerebral palsy. He was a limp vegetable, totally unresponsive to sound or touch. His parents had abandoned him.

The hospital staff didn't know what to do—until a pediatrician mentioned May Lemke, a nurse governess living nearby. A nurse telephoned May and explained that in all likelihood Leslie would die in a short time. "Would you help us by taking care of him while he lives?" the nurse asked.

"If I take him, he certainly will not die, and I will take him," May replied. The nurse never mentioned that the county could provide money for the infant's care, and it never occurred to May to ask.

That was 30 years ago. May was 52 at the time. She and her second husband, Joe, lived in a small house at the edge of a lake in nearby Pewaukee. A World War I bride from England, May had raised five children to adulthood. Her first husband died in 1943, and five years later she married Joe Lemke, a skilled construction worker.

Four and a half feet tall and weighing 90 pounds, May is still the direct-talking, indefatigable woman Joe married. And she retains the same deep faith in God. Today, at 82 she rarely walks; she scurries.

When May accepted the baby, she accepted him as just that, a baby— no different from others—to be taught and loved. On the first feeding attempt, she saw that Leslie lacked the sucking reflex that is spontaneous with most babies. Apparently, he had been fed by tube at the hospital. May quickly taught him. She put the bottle nipple between his lips, then put her lips near his, moving the nipple and making sucking sounds against his cheek. He caught on.

As she worked with him, May sang a lullaby remembered from her own childhood. She changed a few words to fit Leslie's blindness:

Only a baby small dropped from the sky
Only a baby small without any eyes
Only a baby small always at rest
Only a baby small that God knows best.

She bathed him, cuddled him for hours, talked to him, sang to him. He never moved or uttered a sound.

Year after year she cared for him, but there was no movement. No smile. No tears. No sound. If May had not tied him to the back of the chair he would have toppled over.

May never stopped talking to him. She massaged his back, legs, arms, and fingers. She prayed, and sometimes when she prayed she wept and put Leslie's hands to her cheeks so he could feel the tears. "I feel sad right now and I'm crying," she would say.

May refused to consider the child a burden. "I did not seek Leslie, so there has to be a reason why I was picked to raise this child," she told herself. "God in his time will show me the reason."

May was never reluctant to bring Leslie out in public. He was her boy, her love. She intuitively felt that somewhere in the maze of his damaged brain he was trying, and she was proud of him. During a bus ride, a woman who several times had seen May talking to the unresponsive boy in her arms said, "Why don't you put that child in an institution? You're wasting your life."

"It's you who's wasting your life," May snapped. "This kind of a child is brought around by kindness and love. Not in an hour or a month or a year. Lasting kindness and love."

One summer, Joe spent hours in the lake bobbing the boy around in the water, hoping that the doll-like, lifeless movements of his arms and legs would inspire him to move his limbs voluntarily. Once or twice May thought she detected deliberate motions, but Leslie did not repeat them.

That fall May took Leslie to a rehabilitation center in Milwaukee. No one thought anything could be done for the boy. There was not a single word of encouragement.

This professional pessimism didn't deter her. She knew that someday Leslie was going to break out of his prison. She just had to help him. She tried to think of a way to get the concept of walking into his mind. He had never made a move to crawl. He had never seen anyone walk.

She asked Joe, who was a rock of support, to make a wide leather belt for her waist and attach small loops in each side of it. Taking steps, she would clasp Leslie's hands to her hips in the hope that he would absorb the walking motion. He just slumped and dangled beside her.

The Lemkes then had a chain-link fence erected along the side of their property, and May stood Leslie next to it, thrusting his fingers through the openings. After several weeks, he finally got the idea of letting the fence support him. He stood. He was 16.

Then May tried to get him to move along the fence. She never stopped talking to him, encouraging him: "Come on, love, move just a little bit, a little bit." She said this hundreds of times, moving his hands and feet herself. Finally, he moved on his own.

Once he could do that, she tried to lure him away from the fence. "Come to Mamma, love. Please come to Mamma," she'd call. After months, he learned to totter two or three steps.

It was an interminable, grueling struggle, but May never thought of it as a struggle; she was simply striving to help her boy. But she knew that she needed help in this effort. Please do something for Leslie, May prayed time and again. He may be 18 years old, but he's still a baby.

Once she got angry. "The Bible tells of the miracles. Please dear God, let there be a miracle for this boy."

One day she noticed Leslie's index finger moving against a taut piece of string around a package, as if plucking it. Was this a sign? she wondered. What did it mean?

Music! she exclaimed to herself. That's it. Music. From then on the Lemke house was filled with music from the record player, the radio, and the TV. Hour after hour the music played. Leslie gave no indication that he was listening.

May and Joe bought an old upright piano for $250 and placed it in Leslie's bedroom. Repeatedly, May pushed his fingers against the keys to show him that his fingers could make sounds. He remained totally indifferent.

It happened in the winter of 1971. May was awakened by the sound of music. It was 3 a.m. Someone was playing Tchaikovsky's Piano Concerto No. 1. She shook Joe. "Did you leave the radio on?" she asked.

"No," he said.

"Then where's the music coming from?" She swung out of bed and turned on a living room light. It dimly illuminated Leslie's room. Leslie was at the piano. May saw a smile glowing on his face.

He had never before gotten out of bed on his own. He had never seated himself at the piano. He had never voluntarily or deliberately struck the keys with his fingers. Now he was actually playing a concerto—and with deftness and confidence.

May fell to her knees. "Thank you, God. You didn't forget Leslie."

Leslie obviously had been listening to the music, and listening with such intense concentration that, like a computer, his brain had stored every composition that had come to his ears. Why the music burst out of him on that early morning hour in late winter is unknown. But come it did, like a gale. His repertoire ranged through the classics, rock, ragtime, country western, and gospel.

"Coming out" musically opened the door for all kinds of emotions and developments. Occasionally a single word popped from his mouth. Then one afternoon some children were playing on the other side of the chain fence, and May asked them what they were doing. One of them answered.

"We're having fun," he said in a thick but understandable voice. It was his first complete sentence, and May grabbed him and hugged him.

Several months later, in the family living room, Leslie began to tremble, and tears rolled down his cheeks. "I'm crying," he sobbed. "I'm crying." He had never wept before and now he did so just as his mother had years before.

May watched him cry for 20 minutes. She was grateful that he could express whatever pain or fear had been locked inside him. To her it was a beautiful sight.

Leslie also learned to feel his way through the rooms. May and Joe taught him to use the toilet. He brushed his teeth. He bathed himself.

Meanwhile, Leslie's skill at the piano steadily increased. His rendition of Gershwin's "Rhapsody in Blue" is a tour de force, flawless and evocative.

And he sings. Before learning to speak clearly he could readily mimic a variety of singers. He has a big, round voice and, when he pulls out all the stops, it can be heard a block away. He can do Luciano Pavarotti in two Italian operas, Jimmy Durante in "Inka Dinka Doo," Louis Armstrong in "Helly, Dolly!" and both parts of the Jeanette MacDonald-Nelson Eddy duet in "Sweethearts."

Two years ago, at the age of 28, Leslie began talking in earnest. Although he cannot hold a give-and-take conversation, he makes statements and can ask and answer questions. Sometimes he expresses an opinion. While listening to TV one night Leslie got fed up with the dialog in a situation comedy. "Better get that off," he said. "They're all crazy."

As news of Leslie's talent traveled, groups requested him for concerts. May pondered the invitations; then she decided that public appearances would be valuable to Leslie. The music would give him a sense of participating in society.

"And those people sitting out there, watching and listening, might get a sense of wonderment and a feeling of hope that they might never have had. They would see what can happen to a human being thought to be absolutely hopeless and helpless."

Leslie played at churches, civic clubs and schools, and for groups of cerebral palsy and retarded children and their parents. He went on to colleges, county fairs, local television, and finally network television.

He loves performing. Sometimes he will burst into song while sitting in an airport lounge or airliner. People around him are often startled by his first notes, but his closing always is met with exclamations and applause.

There still are many things that Leslie cannot do. Those fingers that perform so brilliantly at the keyboard cannot use a knife or fork. Conversation does not flow easily. But ask what music means to him and he replies with a voice that is firm.

"Music," says Leslie, "is love."

★ ★ ★

For nearly two centuries authorities have puzzled over the phenomenon of the autistic savant (often called idiot savant), a person who, though mentally retarded by brain damage, is capable of an extraordinary specific talent.

"The feats performed by a typical autistic savant are usually far beyond the capabilities of even the most brilliant of normal minds," says Bernard Rimland in *Cognitive Defects in the Development of Mental Illness.* "How can a child with an IQ of 37 instantly tell you that 6,327 times 4,234 equals 27,211,918?"

And Leslie's achievement, especially since it occurred after childhood, is so formidable that it defies belief. "We can neither match the autistic savant's performance nor explain how it is achieved," Rimland, director of the Institute for Child Behavior Research in San Diego, and a leading researcher in the field, further states.

But May Lemke believes there's only one explanation for a miracle. And each day she gives Leslie the same loving care that helped that miracle occur.

Joseph P. Blank

Value Clarification Exercise

1. Make a list of no more than 10 people with whom you would share the rest of your life if for some unknown reason there could be no others. Try to give reasons for your choices of each person on your list.
2. Make a list of no more than 10 careers (job positions) which you would like to have if, for some unknown reason, you learned about your future and discovered that you would change careers (jobs) 10 times in your lifetime. Try to give reasons for your selections and rank your choices in order of amount of interest to you.
3. Make a list of no more than 10 major achievements that you will have (or would like to have) completed in your lifetime if for some unknown reason you were able to predict accurately your future. Try to rank the achievements in order of importance to you and explain the meaning each might have to you.
4. Make a list of no more than 10 principles by which you wish to live your life if for some unknown reason you were expected to present your principles for review before a committee on living. Try to justify the inclusion of each principle in your list and indicate how these principles would be reflected in your behavior.
5. Make a list of no more than 10 people who have had a significant influence on your lifestyle (values, attitudes, behaviors) if for some unknown reason you could choose no others. Try to describe briefly each person and note the characteristics you like and dislike.
6. Make a list of no more than 10 life incidents, situations, or experiences which have had a significant impact on your goals for life and career direction. Try to give reasons for your choice of experiences and note the roles played by other people.
7. Make a list of no more than 10 pieces of music which you would like to keep for life if for some unknown reason you could have no others. Try to give reasons for each selection.

Other topics that might be considered using the same framework as above are:

Historical events
Favorite friends, teachers, bosses
Worldly possessions, articles of value
Places of residence, travel

Conclusion

Do the students really become leaders? Students of good character? Can Character Development and Leadership Training really be taught?

Our program has been in existence for fewer than 10 years now, so I cannot point to any U.S. senators or corporation presidents from our ranks. I am confident, though, that many of our students will go on to experience great success in life, and at least in part because of their experience. I believe we have set them on the correct path. My hope is that in years to come I will have some examples to back up that statement.

We hold reunions on a regular basis. My hope is that in addition to pleasant socializing our alumni will be able to examine their old life-collages and writings (I save all these) in order to measure their personal, academic, and social growth since leaving the course. It has been my observation that the graduates, because of the close-knit team concept of the course, keep in contact with each other even without these formal reunions.

I find that they also—and for the same reasons—keep closer contact with the teacher than with teachers of other subjects. Certainly, my students seem to stay in touch with me more than the students from other courses I have taught.

For the time being, even without a record of adult successes to cite as evidence, I will say without hesitation that a Character Development and Leadership Training class will prove a valuable addition to any school. It is worth the effort.

Make it happen. You will not regret it.